CURTIS GILLESPIE

Someone Like That

life stories

Cover Art: by Nina Haggerty
Cover Design: Priority Printing
Interior Design: McRobbie Design Group
Printed and bound in Canada by Priority Printing, Edmonton

Rowan Books gratefully acknowledges the ongoing support and assistance of:
    SKILLS Training and Support Services Association

SKILLS Training and Support Services Association gratefully acknowledges the support and assistance of:
    Human Rights, Citizenship and Multiculturalism Education Fund
    Edmonton Public Teachers' Charity Trust Fund, Local No. 37 of the
    Alberta Teachers' Association

Rowan Books and SKILLS gratefully acknowledges the support of:
    Debra Wooding, Vice President, Merrill Lynch Canada

Canadian Cataloguing in Publication Data

Gillespie, Curtis, 1960-
Someone like that

ISBN 0-9685257-2-5

1. Developmentally disabled—Alberta—Biography. I. Title.
HV1570.5.C32A55 2000 362.1'968'0097123 C00-910330-9

Published in Canada by
Rowan Books Inc.
#410, 10113 - 104 St. Edmonton, AB T5J 1A1
(780) 421-1544

ALSO BY CURTIS GILLESPIE

The Progress of an Object in Motion

*This book is dedicated to the memory of Pauline Morin,
who believed in the project from the start, and to
Rose Stewart, whose passing inspired it.*

PREFACE

Seeing this book grow from vision to reality has been an amazing experience. In 1996, I sat in a small chapel in Edmonton, listening as a support worker struggled to contain her emotion as she read the eulogy she had written for Rose Stewart. I had "known" Rose – a tiny woman, confined to her bed, unable to speak, see or care for herself. How had this woman inspired such obvious love and affection from those around her?

I heard her story that day, for the first and last time. She had a history, a life, and I wished that I could have known her as these people did. As I listened, and learned, and regretted, I looked around the room and saw other faces – Jessie, Emil, Germaine. They too have rich stories – histories – but already they were becoming lost to time and faded memory. It became important, in that moment, that their life stories not be lost.

I am grateful to Curtis Gillespie for his immediate and unfailing enthusiasm for the idea behind this book, for his gifted writing, and for his friendship. He has given the individuals whose stories are told here a very special and enduring gift – their histories.

I would also like to thank Rowan Books, SKILLS' Board of Directors, and the staff who have helped with the writing of these stories for their generosity of time and spirit.

– Wendy Hollo, April 2000 –

INTRODUCTION

Persons with developmental disabilities have for too long been seen as non-citizens, people who need to be cared for and kept out of sight rather than as people that add to society's richness – a burden as opposed to a benefit. Such attitudes are thankfully changing, and this book is part of that process. To have known people who have been denied even a shred of self-determination – because they were confined to institutions or given no rights in the community – provokes anger and sadness, but also the desire to get things right. There is therefore a moral statement to be made by this book's very existence, and it is this: persons with developmental disabilities must not be denied ownership of their pasts and futures. It's that simple.

I have received enormous assistance from many people throughout the course of years that it took to bring this book to completion. They are too many to name individually, but certainly every person named in this book should know that it could not have been written without their assistance and their spirit. A special thank you must go to Wendy Hollo, the Executive Director of SKILLS (an Edmonton social services agency which is frequently referred to throughout the book in those terms only). This book was her idea. I have been friends with Wendy for many years, and I'm honoured that she asked me to be part of her vision. It was her determination that made this book a reality. Thanks too, to Heather and Debbie at Rowan Books for their care and attention to the manuscript. I'd also like to thank my wife Cathy and my daughters, Jessica and Grace, for the love I have in my house.

Finally, I want to thank eight people who possess no small degree of humour, courage and will. Davie, Germaine, Jessie, Emil, Karen, Ron, Rita and Nina. I feel deeply fortunate to have come to know them and to have heard their stories. I hope you feel the same.

– Curtis Gillespie, April 2000 –

CONTENTS

Someone Like That

life stories

The Wall

T he Wall, Pink Floyd's seminal 1979 concept album, rumbles out of the speakers, and Ron Randall is listening intently. We don't need no thought control, sings Roger Waters. No dark sarcasm in the classroom. Ron lip-synchs along. He knows the words. He knows the music. More than anything else, he knows and understands the story, this riveting rock-narrative that documents the injustices children suffer at the hands of so many. Ron and I are almost exactly the same age, and I can remember when The Wall was released. I was just as captivated as he was and is now. Listening to the music with him not only reminds me of my own late teen years, but it helps me hear the music all over again, because I'm hearing it through his ears, listening to it to try and hear what he hears. It's more poignant than it has ever been, stronger and also a little darker. Ron has a developmental disability, but has also been functionally blind from birth through the effects of cataracts.

The music spills from the speakers of his massive CD player, and Ron moves, shuffles, shakes, gestures. It becomes clear as I listen to the music and watch Ron listening to the music, that it's more than just something he listens to. This music means something to him, not just about life in general terms, but about his life. Ron is a sharp thinker. He can be clear and to the point, and he understands the meaning of this music at its most fundamental, which is that oppression is oppression, no matter what you call it, and that early oppression leads to deeply troubled human beings. The intensity of Ron's attraction to drama is on display here. He loves narrative, he loves intrigue, he loves drama. If there's any question you ever want answered about Pink Floyd, just ask Ron. He's a deep well of information, but it's the storytelling in the music he really loves. Deep down Ron is a storyteller himself, though there will always be aspects of his own story that will remain part of the buried past.

∞

Ron was born in May of 1960 in Edmonton at the Royal Alexandra Hospital. His family lived in St. Albert, which is where he was raised until about the age of ten. Exact dates are hazy for Ron, but his younger sister Alison remembers that age ten is about right. This was the age at which Ron's father moved him to Brantford to attend a residential school for the blind. Nobody in the family can ever remember Ron's dad saying exactly why he sent him away, but the reasons seem fairly straightforward. Ron's mother and father split up around this time. There was also considerable pressure on Ron's father at home, since he raised all five children on his own after he and his wife separated.

And so he made the decision to send Ron away. This began a period in Ron's life that was not happy by any stretch of the imagination. In fact, Ron has banished most of it from his memory, and recalls only images and bare snippets of events. Alison does remember one thing Ron picked up while in Brantford that he loved, and which he still talks about sometimes. That was ham radio. "He became quite amazing at it, actually," says Alison. "I wouldn't be surprised if he picked it up again some day."

Ron remembers that he had adversaries at his residential school. There were children who made fun of him, likely because he had a developmental disability on top of his visual impairment. While at the Brantford school, Ron lived in a general dormitory. He remembers one fellow schoolmate in particular, a fellow who tried to drown Ron in a swimming pool when they were in their mid-teens. "I do not know what his problem was," Ron says to this day, shaking his head slowly at the memory of it.

The discord was heavy within his family at this time, as well. Ron remembers his mother telling him that his father was alcoholic, but he never knew for sure if it was true. He doesn't have a lot of memories of his father, since he left home when he was ten and didn't come back until he was nearly eighteen. He lived with his father for the next five years, but then in 1982 his father, who was fifty-two, passed away. "I knew my Dad only a little bit," says Ron, gazing sightlessly at me as he speaks.

Still, not everything was grim for Ron during those early years. Before he went off to Brantford, Alison certainly remembers Ron as being willfull. She laughs when she tells the story that for her exemplifies just how independent-minded Ron was when he was a child. When he was seven years old, just to show everyone how independent he could be, he walked off to the playground closest to their house in St Albert. "And it wasn't like it was just across the alley," laughs Alison. "Nobody could find him and we were starting to panic a bit. He wasn't around the house or the yard, so we decided to look around the neighbourhood. Well, the playground was across the street, up a full block, then in half a block, down a kind of cul-de-sac. Obviously, he knew the way by memory from all the times we'd taken him there. It was incredible."

Ron just decided to go to the playground and then simply went. He didn't tell anyone or ask anyone to go with him. He just set out, a blind seven-year-old boy with a developmental disability.

"He wasn't anywhere else," says Alison, "and when we finally looked in the playground, there he was, checking out all the stuff. It was amazing."

Ron also used to zip around the neighbourhood on his green tricycle. He'd done it so many times, he knew every crack in the sidewalk, every little bump that indicated a driveway. "Oh, yes," says Ron, in the hoarse whisper that is his normal speaking voice. "I knew every little bump along the way."

"He liked to swim a lot back then, and even won medals for his swimming as a teenager. He used to love the big water slide in Kelowna, too," says Alison, smiling and shaking her head at the memories. "But then he liked the scary thrill stuff, too, so it wasn't all that surprising. He was quite an independent little guy."

The Tim Hortons is crowded today, but we still manage to find a table. Pretty soon Ron is on a roll, telling me about some of the things he finds funny. Ron loves comedians, and is particularly fond of Bill Cosby and Cheech & Chong. Then he lists some of the TV programs he likes to listen in on. "Montel," he says, grinning. "And Maury Povich, too. I love it when the guests start scrapping like cats and dogs, and Maury has to get them to calm down or he sends them to boot camp."

Jane Steblyk, who has worked with Ron for five years now, laughs. "And he gets a kick out of the commercials, too." She turns to Ron and smiles at him. "Don't you, Ron?"

Ron rotates his head in mock disgust. "Oh, some of those commercials. They drive me crazy."

Pretty soon, Jane is urging Ron to do an imitation for me. He demurs briefly, putting up a token resistance before launching into an imitation of Popeye from a soup commercial that has been running a lot lately. In the middle of the Tim Hortons he breaks out into a perfect, and loud, imitation of Popeye rescuing Olive Oyl from the train tracks. His intonation is perfect, as is his sense of drama. So much so that people from some of the nearby tables glance up to see what our laughter is about. They get the gist and laugh along too.

Next, he wants to tell me about some of his favourite singers. One of his favourites is Stevie Wonder. In fact, he tells me of a dream he had recently that involved Stevie Wonder.

"Yeah," he says conspiratorially. "I was living at a different house. Not the house I'm living in now. I was having a bath. And then there was a knock on the door. Someone answered it and then came in to the bathroom, and said, 'Ron, you have a special guest.' It was Stevie Wonder. He was there to visit me. But I said, 'Oh, I'm in the bath.'"

Ron rotates his head around the coffee shop for a second, then turns his face back to ours. "I don't know what that means."

Neither myself nor Jane can help Ron out with that one, so we press on to matters of considerably greater importance. Namely, talking about record stores which along with the library are Ron's favourite places to go to pick up new music. He loves Pink Floyd, of course, and the Beatles. But he doesn't listen only to pop and rock classics. He thinks Weird Al Yankovic is great, and he was recently introduced to a group called Mr. Bungo, which is half polka and half rock and roll. "They're great," he enthuses. "And weird." Ron is also a great fan of live music, and has gone to many concerts. Ken Johnston, a staff person at the residence, remembers that a thrill for Ron was going to see the Edmonton group Jr. Gone Wild in a local bar and meeting them afterwards. He's even taken some keyboard lessons.

Jane laughs and tells me about the time they all went to the library, and one of the staff pulled a little practical joke on Ron by slipping a Partridge Family CD into his library bag. Unsuspectingly, he went home and put it on. When he heard David Cassidy singing *I Think I Love You*, he along with everyone else in the apartment burst out laughing.

℃

Ron has a strong faith, and it's been getting stronger these last few years. Most recently he's been listening to Christian shows on the radio. He listens to the many Bible tapes he has, primarily, he says, because he's trying to have some confidence in what the Bible has to say. These are things Ron thinks about at length. He would love to get a Braille Bible, though they tend to be about six feet thick. He attends Christ Church Meadows with Ross, one of the weekend staff who also happens to be visually impaired. Alison says that over the years she's noticed Ron has taken on a slightly different set of values from hers when it comes to religion. "He's starting to get quite…positional," she smiles. At family dinners Ron, who was baptized Lutheran, will often say grace.

When I ask Ron what it was that he liked about Christ Church Meadows, his response is quick. "The drama!" he says. It was the last thing you might expect to hear as a reason for going to church, but in getting to know Ron, and learning more about the church itself, it made more and more sense. The pastors and lay people at Christ Church Meadows will often act out readings from the scripture. The church's choice to make theatre out of the Bible fits right in with Ron's attraction to drama and narrative. The truth is, if Ron had had a different background or upbringing he might have become an actor or a writer himself, since these pursuits so consistently deal with the conflict of human drama, family, love, death, relationships.

"Oh, no question," says Jane, grinning. "If Ron ever overhears anyone having a squabble, he gets quite interested, as long as he doesn't have to get involved himself. He loves conflict as long as he doesn't have to get in the thick of it. Even when he hears the TV or the movies warning that 'viewer discretion is advised' he perks up."

"Ron does like to live life on the edge a bit," says Deb

Huber, an agency Program Manager. She's known Ron since he came to the agency ten years ago. "A little crisis in his day gives him something to worry about. He's always had a sort of quiet intensity to him, and after you get to know him, you really start to see just how insightful he is about people."

℘

The last ten years have generally been very good for Ron, but his time in the community has not always had the stability it has now. Ron lived with his father for five years after Brantford, from 1977 to 1982. After that he moved into a city–run residential setting, a large dorm-style group home that he didn't enjoy. He stayed there briefly, moving in 1983 to a group home where he was somewhat happier, though he still chafed against the restrictions of the era and the setting. He remained there until 1988, after which he lived for two years in a supported residence run by yet another local agency. Finally, in 1990, Ron moved into a more independent residential setting, one he still enjoys today.

Deb Huber remembers that when Ron first moved in he had almost no structure to his day or his life. He was up until two in the morning, and would sleep until noon the next day. It was a case of almost total physical care, care that included the staff handling all his cooking and cleaning. He was inactive in virtually every aspect of his life due, thinks Deb, to the request of both Ron and his family not to push him to do anything. Getting Ron into some sort of routine was crucial. The staff encouraged him to make an investment in himself, to take some responsibility. "It was gradual," says Deb. "But it did work." Nowadays, Ron gets out a lot more than he ever has; he does his laundry, he even does some of his cooking. And though his cooking is certainly improving, Ron still laughs noting that that toaster somehow manages to burn a couple pieces of his toast every day. These days he can fry up a pretty tasty pork chop and add in a little rice and corn. Once, he even baked a chicken.

"He's had to learn a lot of these things gradually," says Deb. "But he's also learned a great deal in the last decade about his rights and responsibilities. That's been so important."

The support and stability of Alison has also been very important to Ron, as has a concept that is still relatively new to him, a concept so many of us take for granted, privacy. This is one of the key elements for Ron when asked what he likes about living in the community. "Privacy," he says forcefully. "Privacy is one thing I love about my apartment." Years of growing up in dorms and huge group homes undoubtedly looms large in Ron's mind as he talks about how he cherishes his privacy. The one thing that can be said for certain about the majority of institutions is that they are designed with the eradication of privacy in mind.

Of course, in his typically sardonic way, Ron can also tell you what he doesn't like about living in an apartment with just one roommate – hockey. His roommate Dan loves the Edmonton Oilers, but not Ron. "I really don't care who wins. Not even when it's the Oilers. They're all just a bunch of big shots who make too much money." Fortunately, Ron notes, he always has his bedroom to retreat to if the hockey game gets too loud. His boom box can overcome the sound of any play-by-play.

Ron also likes to go to the movies on Saturdays, and he remembers, too, what a blast he had last year when he went on a "holiday" to West Edmonton Mall. He stayed in the Igloo room, a theme room at the Fantasyland Hotel, and swam in the wave pool. "I felt like a cork in a bottle," he laughs. He went to a movie and did some CD shopping. "I'd like to go back and stay there someday." He prefers it to Cuba, where his mother once took him for a vacation. "Oh, it was a crazy hotel, there were dogs all over the place, and I was afraid of sharks in the water. Cuba was not paradise," nods Ron. "Only heaven is paradise."

When you ask Deb Huber what comes to mind when she thinks of Ron, the first thing that pops into her mind, of course, is his music. The second thing is that to her, and others, Ron is very much a thinker. "It's not so much that he'll give you a quick answer, but that he will always think about what it is that he wants to say." She also loves his sense of humour and his imitations. "Basically," says Deb, "I think he just wants to be a regular guy." Ron has never really been too involved with the disabled community. He doesn't want to be treated differently from anyone else out there. But this might be hard for Ron to fully realize. "I think a lot of his disability in growing up was just with a lack of confidence," Deb says. "Maybe that's still the case."

Even though Ron's life in the community is improving continually, there are still moments when the community at large butts its head up against the differentness of some of its citizens. And as we know, Ron does not like confrontation of any sort, or at least not any confrontation he's involved in! It's great when it's on Montel or Jerry Springer, but not when it's his own life. He remembers once walking down the sidewalk on Jasper Avenue and accidentally running into somebody standing waiting for the bus. He tried to explain that he was visually impaired. "She didn't care. I said, 'excuse me,' trying to be polite. 'You clown,' she said to me. What was her problem? I didn't ask. I just whacked her with my cane." For a moment I take Ron seriously until a grin leaks out onto his face.

଼

As Ron and I listen to the last couple of songs of the first side of The Wall we are so intent on the music that we've almost stopped speaking. During the next-to-last song, *Another Brick in the Wall, Part 3*, it becomes clear that Ron doesn't just listen to his music for the pleasure it gives him, though there can be no doubt that one of the joys of Ron's life is the music that gets inside his head, the music that so moves him. And it's also true that he doesn't just listen to his music for the vivid worlds it creates for him, the stories that are told that only he can see inside. These are stories that must take place in his head in a form those of us without a visual impairment can never understand. It's not about better or worse, it's about one's reality. Ron has not once complained about his blindness to me, or said he wishes things were different. Nor should he.

No, Ron's music is not just about these things. It's also a powerful statement. He's telling me who he is. This is how he's choosing to do it.

"Quite an independent little guy," Alison says of Ron as a child. Not much has changed. With all that he's been through since he was a seven-year-old blithely riding around the neighbourhood on his green tricycle – the boarding school, the family turmoil, the difficulties of integration, the loneliness – Ron still fiercely desires independence, but he lives in a world where

13

society forces a level of dependence upon him. Ron and I sit listening as Roger Waters of Pink Flyod sings that he doesn't need arms to hold him, or drugs to calm him. The writing's on the wall, sings Waters and he doesn't need anything at all.

Ron has chosen to play this music for me. Not just anything, but this specifically. He's not saying so, but I know he's speaking to me through it, in the same way that so many people with disabilities need to find unique and new ways to express what it is they have to say. If we really did want to understand, all we would have to do is stop and listen. So why don't we?

Ron Randall

Photo by J. Steblyk, 2000

The Field

Ha Ha!

There comes a moment while listening to Germaine Toutant singing and playing the piano, when I am reminded again of the value of each and every human life. As I listen to her play, I think to myself that it doesn't matter what the circumstances are, what abilities a person has, what rights or wrongs their pasts contain. What matters is that one single person is a whole world, a world of talents, hopes, fears, and loves, and that these complex characteristics ought to be celebrated. I'm thinking all this while Slim Whitman is warbling and cooing on the record player, music to which Germaine is playing along on the piano. She has nearly perfect pitch. She knows the words. She sings in tune. Her eyes are slightly closed and she's concentrating, but in a way that suggests it's less concentration than a kind of rapture. The song ends. She smiles nervously, wondering if I liked the song.

"Amazing," I reply.

"Ha, ha!" she says, grinning impishly, her eyes lit up behind her thick glasses. This, one soon learns being around Germaine, is her trademark. Ha, ha! The note of triumph, or of having good-naturedly pulled the wool over your eyes. If she thinks she's got one on you, her eyes glitter like flashlights. Ha, ha!

"I can play something else, you know," she says, her nervousness disappearing. "I can play anything, if I can just hear it first."

Germaine's singing and piano playing is a source of wonder. She's that good. Her father, Leo, who was an oil well worker, a barber and a trucker, was also very musical. He played the piano and the banjo. Germaine's brother Ron was a singer when they were growing up, and he still has his deep contra-bass voice.

"Even from the start," says Ron, who now lives in British Columbia, "Germaine had a great ear, and excellent pitch. We didn't have TV in those days, so we did a lot of singing as a family, a lot of harmonizing. Germaine was great at harmony, she could do it right away."

Germaine sang from about the age of 10, and a couple of years after that started tinkling away at the piano. She is self-taught. Her father was often away working, and given the fact that she had little else to do for long stretches of time, Germaine simply decided to teach herself how to play.

"She definitely did it on her own," says Ron, laughing. "She's so stubborn, she wouldn't have ever let someone else teach her how to do it!"

Germaine's love and facility for music is remembered even by people who don't see her much anymore. Lois and George Stewart are the parents of Rose Stewart, a woman who lived in the same residence with Germaine for many years. Rose and Germaine were close friends until Rose passed away in 1996. "I will always remember Germaine," says Lois. "She is such a good singer. She used to come with Rose, George and myself to Ebenezer United Church, and I was always amazed at how she could sing. She knew the words to all the hymns, and could sing them just perfectly.

And even though Germaine is such an independent person, she and Rose always got along. Rose and Germaine just seemed to have a kind of way together. Another thing I'll always remember about Germaine," says Lois, laughing, "is how strong she likes her tea. Oh, my goodness, she likes it strong. She used to come visit us with Rose. I like my tea fairly weak, so we'd always have to make a special pot for Germaine because she liked it so strong."

ॐ

Germaine is 63 years old now. She lives in a supported residence in the Westmount area of Edmonton. She's been there for over ten years, and there can be almost no doubt that right now is the happiest time of Germaine's life. She was born on the 26th of August, 1936 in Edmonton, and has lived there all her life. She lived with her parents until 1983, when her mother became seriously ill. At that point, Germaine moved into the Lynnwood Continuing Care facility in Edmonton. It's hard for any of us to imagine what that must have been like for Germaine, to have lived in the family home for forty seven years, and to then suddenly find oneself in the community. She lived at Lynnwood for three years. Besides the multitude of adjustments she was forced to make during this time, both her parents passed away; her mother in 1984 and her father in 1986. Even though her mother passed away in 1984, she had been ill for the previous ten years. It was, says Germaine's sister Judy, their father that really cared for Germaine from the early 1970s until she moved to Lynnwood in 1983. Germaine remained at Lynnwood until 1986, at which point she moved into the Westmount residence, where she's been ever since.

The person Germaine is closest to nowadays is probably her younger sister, Judy. There were four kids altogether: Germaine the oldest, followed by Ron, Ken and then Judy. Their mother was a school teacher, and it must have rubbed off, because all three of Germaine's siblings have worked in the school system, two, Judy and Ron as teachers, and one, Ken as an administrator. Both Ron and Judy are candid when they recall that Germaine's childhood was not all sunshine and roses.

"What I really remember most clearly about our lives as children," says Judy, who still lives in Edmonton, "was that Germaine was just always at home. She never went out. Mom and Dad didn't really have much of a life, either. They loved Germaine so much, but they were both so overprotective. Mom was just one of those people who would look at Germaine trying to do things or trying to grow as a person, and would say, 'Oh, it's just easier for me to do it,' and she'd do everything for Germaine."

The irony of this is lost on no one. The one thing so many people with disabilities lack is close involvement with family, yet it was precisely this which stunted Germaine's progress. Her physical limitations were also more severe then than they are now. Her brother Ron remembers that she used to have frequent grand mal seizures which newer medications have helped bring under control. Also, her vision was so bad it hampered her greatly until she had a suitable pair of glasses.

"And of course, she really was overprotected," says Ron. "Too much so right from the start."

Judy agrees. "Mom and Dad decided to keep Germaine with them, but she hardly ever left the house because Mother was always so scared something was going to happen to her." Judy states it most clearly when she says, "For me, when I look back at it, I would say that Germaine's life then was not wonderful."

℞

Sometimes Germaine doesn't hear that well, but she is usually pretty playful and good-humoured about it. One day, Germaine, her support worker Dawn Coull and myself were at a restaurant having a coffee. We got talking about bowling, since that's what we'd gone to the mall to do only to find there were no five-pin lanes available.

"I like bowling," said Germaine, "but I'm not sure how good I am."

"I'm sure I'm worse," I said.

Inexplicably, Germaine grabbed her purse and hid it under the table. She winked at me. "Ha, ha! You wouldn't have the nerve, young fella!"

Dawn and I looked at one another, a little confused.

"You're not getting near my purse," said Germaine, laughing at me, pointing a taunting finger. "You wouldn't have the nerve to steal my purse."

"Steal your purse? I said, I'm sure I'm worse."

We all stared at one another for five seconds, before

bursting into laughter. Ten minutes of sore-stomached, teary-eyed laughter followed, with Germaine leading the way. "Oh, my," she laughed, her eyes wet, her coffee shaking. "Oh, that was a good one." She could hardly control herself and had to put her coffee down, she was laughing so hard. She took her glasses off to wipe her eyes.

"Oh my," she said. "That was a good one. I thought you said you were going to steal my purse. Ha, ha!"

We kept on chuckling for a few more minutes, but the funniest thing of all was that Germaine never did put her purse back on the table.

୫

Compiling a personal history is always difficult as family members pass on. It's even more difficult when the person whose history is being reconstructed, in this case Germaine's, has never been encouraged to remember her own history. Very little documentation remains concerning Germaine's early years. The reminiscences of her siblings Judy and Ron are all we have to go on. Germaine herself remembers almost nothing of her childhood; this may be selective memory, or it could be the result of a stroke she suffered some years ago.

Germaine, as mentioned, lived at home most of her life. While doing so, there were very few attempts made to work with her on education or any real sort of skill building. It was just never a priority. Germaine did attend the Sight Impaired School, which was run out of Garneau School during the Second World War. She did well there, but this was the only opportunity she had to attend school. Values were different 45 years ago.

Another issue Germaine had to deal with, primarily as a witness, was the difficult marriage of her parents. Judy has said that their parents did not always have the best of relationships and that things sometimes got antagonistic. She has also said that alcoholism was an issue in their household – their father had a drinking problem, which was hard on everybody but most notably on their mother. The pressure seems to have gotten to Germaine. At one point, she overdosed on Phenobarbital and had to be taken to Emergency. She was also given to making occasional suicidal remarks during this phase of her life. Happily, as everybody who knows Germaine can attest, she no longer has such thoughts. She is always either in a good mood, or is amiably grousing about what is bothering her.

ප

Germaine has certainly changed over the last decade. Once possessed of a ferociously bad temper, she would often do things almost in spite of her own best interests. She would throw away purses with money in them, or rip money up and throw it in the garbage. Every now and then she would march out into the backyard to suntan in the nude, just because she wanted to, and there was no reason why she thought she shouldn't. It was that simple to her, though she did once try to do it in the middle of 127th Street.

"It used to be quite a challenge to get her to put some clothes on," laughs Marion Bulger, the Westmount residence supervisor. "She just didn't care what other people thought."

Although she is more circumspect today, Germaine is still very much her own person. She recently played an important role in an agency video project demonstrating the extent and variety of the rights people with developmental disabilities have, both in their place of residence and in the community. Germaine sat on the Organizing Committee and was a key figure onscreen, as well.

As she's been given the room to grow, Germaine has blossomed. She's become a more diplomatic person and is taking on a higher level of responsibility for her actions and for herself. She is also learning generosity. The staff at one time did many things for Germaine, but she's learned to do many of these things on her own. There's no denying she can be stubborn, but she is becoming a warmer soul with every passing day.

A few weeks after starting to work with Germaine, I went to the Associated Canadian Travellers (ACT) Recreation Centre with her and her house mates to do some ballroom dancing. I'd been there before, and couldn't wait to get back, such was the sense of fun and ease and warmth that pervades the place when the Elks band strikes up an old Cole Porter tune. On the first waltz I asked Germaine to dance. As we glided across the floor, I noticed that Germaine seemed to be talking to herself.

"What are you saying?" I asked.

She looked up at me, the expression on her face indicating that I was something of a nitwit. "I'm singing the lyrics," she said matter-of-factly.

It was an old show tune from the forties, one whose name I can't remember, but I asked Germaine to sing a little louder so I could hear the words. She did so, and she had the song down pat. Not only that, her pitch and voice were nearly perfect. She could have been up there singing for the crowd. Two weeks later, she did just that, crooning out some songs for everybody's enjoyment. And this is not Germaine's only performance experience. She has been a volunteer at Norwood Continuing Care for over three years, where she plays piano for anyone that wants to come listen. She has become such a well-liked figure at Norwood that she was honoured with a Volunteer Award in April of 1998.

୫

Over the years, Germaine's health has been sporadic. She's suffered from a series of seizures over the years, but these seem to have lessened somewhat, to the point where she only has a minor seizure once every few days. She has also had some psychosis to grapple with, on top of her mental disability. This may have partly explained her temper problems from earlier in her life, although Marion Bulger thinks otherwise. "We've always believed that a lot of the anger and violent tendencies of the past arose from the fact that she is such an independent person," says Marion. "She thinks independently, she wants to be independent, she wants to be her own person. And those times where she can't do something or is restricted in any way due to being a person with a disability, well, she reacts to that. It's easy to understand the frustration she feels sometimes."

"Germaine is a very smart lady," says Germaine's sister Judy, concurring with Marion. "This was even a bit of a problem, in fact, because one of the doctors used to say that she lacked the necessary skills to allow her to live more independently, but that she was easily smart enough and aware enough to look at her siblings, for instance, and see that she was missing out on certain things. Germaine used to tell me sometimes that she wished she could marry or have kids."

Even to this day, Germaine will say things like, "It's hard to find a good man to date," and may even say it to someone she doesn't know that well. It's funny when she says it, and she means it to be comical, but you weep inside, too, because part of Germaine means it seriously. She saw her little sister Judy get married and have three children. Germaine won't have that chance, the chance to be a mother, a wife.

Germaine rarely has temper issues anymore, and has worked hard at learning to control her anger. Outbursts are uncommon, and one thing about Germaine that everybody notices and loves, is the delight she takes in so many ordinary everyday things. She lets out her little giggle, her eyes twinkle. And it can come through the simplest things. Like the time she was out at a movie and went to the washroom, where she noticed for the first time those fancy new hand dryers that blow hot air.

"Oh, she loved that!" laughs Marion. "She talked about that for months."

Germaine has always loved the first day of spring. Not a winter person by any stretch of the imagination, Germaine seems to bloom when winter finally starts to disappear and summer is around the corner. She also loves grocery shopping day. She likes to supervise the unloading of the groceries, and will check all the food that's been bought. She teases the staff. "Boy, look at that!" she'll exclaim. "You've bought up the whole store!"

Germaine was recently given a new TV by Judy, and she enjoys it, but it's a sign of her will and independence that she won't let even something like a TV dictate to her what she'll watch or not watch. She used to enjoy watching *The Price is Right*, but grew so frustrated with the commercials, that she decided to just give it up, to simply go cold turkey. She hasn't watched the show since.

Never having been a person who can be rushed, Germaine tends to enjoy an unhurried pace to her day. She likes to have things to do, but she doesn't like a lot of structure, and whatever structure is attached to her day arises because she's placed it there. She likes to get up in the mornings, make some coffee, read the *Edmonton Journal* through the course of the day, watch some of her favourite TV shows, and make the occasional cup of tea. Sometimes she likes to go out for lunch or to do some shopping.

Germaine can also be very funny when the residential staff attempt to get her involved in things that are not part of her pre-set routine, the routine she's set for herself. Her belief is that staff get paid for a reason, darn it all, and that it's their job, for instance, to cook her dinner! As Dawn Coull says, laughing, "She thinks we're crazy for asking her to help out."

But still, Germaine enjoys doing her own laundry, her own ironing and cleaning her bedroom. This is her domain, and that's the way she's set it up, so it's okay. She takes care of the personal needs she wants to take care of, and if there are things she wants the staff to do, well, that's just the way it's supposed to be!

∞

Growing up, Judy thought very little about the fact that her big sister, Germaine, was "different." She was just part of the family, just one of the kids, although it was obvious that she had other things to worry about, like her eyesight, which hampered her whole adolescence. The family lived in Edmonton's

Garneau and Parkview communities during the five decades Germaine was with her parents. As mentioned earlier, during the last ten years she was at home, it was essentially her father who cared for her.

"In fact," says Judy, "Dad didn't even work during that time, because he spent all his time looking after Germaine, while Mom was teaching school. But our parents, I think, suffered too for keeping Germaine at home so long. Germaine didn't totally benefit from it, but neither did they. It was hard on my Mom all those years when she was ill. We all decided together that Germaine should try Lynnwood. That was the toughest thing on everybody, having her move out."

Judy remembers that while Germaine was at home, her mother could have had Germaine further her education. That might have helped, but her mother chose not to do so. This may explain why Germaine went through such long stretches of her life with little or no social skills. She had problems with the structure at Lynnwood, and it wasn't until she moved into a supported residential setting that she really started to develop an ability to get along with others and to become more outgoing. After all, her parents rarely took Germaine into the community. It wasn't so much embarrassment, Judy recalls, as much as it was just the inconvenience her parents felt they went through. Also, they worried that some terrible fate might befall Germaine. By keeping her in the house, she would at least be safe.

Today, it is primarily Judy out of the three siblings who spends the most time with Germaine. Both Ron and Ken live far away, in B.C. and Ontario respectively, and it's hard for them to see her much.

"The boys didn't always have patience with her, either," says Judy. "But we all had a difficult time growing up, and they left the house early. I can't blame them. Our household was so strict. Especially Mom. These were not particularly happy childhoods at our house."

Knowing this makes Germaine's happiness now all the more worth cherishing. She has some satisfaction with her life, has experienced some genuine growth in which she takes great pride. She derives so much pleasure from life now, from both the little things and the big things.

"It is amazing how happy she is now," concurs Judy. "It's wonderful. I mean, even just the travel. She never went anywhere, and neither did Mom or Dad. We got them all to go to Florida with my husband and kids and myself one year, about 25 years ago. Other than that, nothing. Now, even in the last five years, Germaine has been to B.C., to California, all over the place."

Everybody agrees that what has made the difference in Germaine's life is just being exposed to the outside world that she was sheltered from for so long. This has been crucial to Germaine. Her delight in those little things – grocery shopping, hand dryers, a cup of coffee out, dancing at the ACT – is easy to understand when looked at in this light.

"It's so wonderful, but there's a sad part to it, too," says Judy. "Because if my parents could see her now, they'd see a totally different person than from ten years ago. They'd be amazed. Her life is so positive now. She has friends, she likes where she lives, she travels. They never saw this."

Playing cribbage with Germaine is great fun, but you'd better be on your toes. She shuffles well, deals carefully, arranges her cards in her hand. She scores a dozen on her first hand. She giggles and points to the board. "Look at that," she says. "I'm ahead of you. Ha, ha!"

She's having fun, and in between games she can't wait for the next one to start, which strikes me as a wonderful symbol of where Germaine is at right now. The future is a place Germaine isn't scared to go. She might cut back on a few of her volunteer activities, because she doesn't want to overdo things, even though she is getting more exercise than she ever has. She's doing as much walking as she can, and the staff at the house want to make Germaine's health and fitness the big priority. She'll be 64 this year, after all.

"I remember the doctors from when Germaine was young," says Ron. "They said Germaine wouldn't even live to be forty. I guess she's proved them wrong. There's no doubt she suffered a bit for staying in the house so much. I don't know, maybe our mother did feel some of the stigma of Germaine's condition and that made her the way she was. Germaine simply wasn't happy then, but I'll tell you, she's sure a lot happier now."

Germaine deals the cards again, counting them carefully. She neatly arranges them in her hand then turns her face up to mine, waiting for me to play, practically squirming in her seat waiting for me to make my first mistake. It doesn't take long. She puts down a card to follow my own. "Fifteen for two!" she declares, moving her peg. "Two points."

"Shoot!" I say.

Germaine stares at me for only a second before it comes out, and when it does, I can't help but grin. It's almost worth making mistakes on purpose just to hear it.

"Two points," she says. "Ha, ha!"

Germaine Toutant

Photo by Sears™, 1999

Poppies

Inside I Was Screaming

The only proper response is outrage. Sadness follows, and only when this has passed through your system can you find the room to feel some joy. Rita and Nina Haggerty might have found a space for some peace and happiness in their last years, but it's the first seventy years of their lives that bring a lump to the throat and the hot flush of collective shame to one's face. It was our society, after all, in which this happened. Most of us complain about losing our memory, but how many injustices must you suffer to complain that you remember too much? The memory banks of Rita and Nina were obscenely overcrowded, crammed with enough nightmares to fill more than their own lifetimes. And now both are gone.

Their lives began peaceably enough. Rita was born in 1915 and Nina in 1916, both in Edmonton, Alberta. Their mother was widowed during the first World War, and Rita and Nina never saw their biological father. After the Great War, their mother took domestic work so she could be at home with her two little girls.

It was when Rita was nine that the "sky fell in," as one of Rita's church companions, Rosie Pflederer, puts it. Both girls contracted polio, and Rita got the worst of it. Her limbs slowly but inescapably folded in and tightened up, like a fresh pretzel drying in the sun. Her arms crossed over her chest and her legs began to draw up over her arms.

Their mother was frantic, terrified. She wrote to Sister Kenney in England, who was at that time the only real authority on polio. Hydrotherapy was suggested, but an aunt of the girls worked at the Mayo Clinic in Rochester, Minnesota, and their mother decided to see what could be done there. Sympathetic neighbours chipped in to help defray the costs of the trip. At the Mayo Clinic a doctor who recognized that nothing else could be done straightened out Rita's feet and then cut the tendons in her groin muscles so that her legs would unfold. She would never walk normally again, but at least now she could use crutches. Slowly, the lives of the Haggerty women began to stabilize.

However, their mother met a man while they were in Minnesota. His name is not known to us, and very little is known about him. They courted, fell in love and married. They remained in Minnesota. "He seemed like an answer to her prayers," says Rosie Pflederer, "after all those years of drudgery, loneliness and worry."

Their honeymoon was brief. Rita's and Nina's mother did not know she'd married an alcoholic. When he drank he turned violent and dangerous, sometimes disappearing for weeks on end, sometimes returning broke and spitting mad about things they couldn't understand and which he couldn't explain.

Not long after they'd begun living in Minnesota together as a family, Nina overheard her mother and stepfather arguing. Her mother was crying, begging for some money to spend on some essentials for the girls. Rita, who was a clever girl, knew about the suspicious bulge in her parents mattress. While the adults argued, she went upstairs and began hacking at the mattress with a pair of scissors. Money spilled from the wounded bed, but as Rita was scooping it up to take it to her mother, her stepfather slipped into the room behind her. Insane with anger, he picked her up, crutches, braces and all, and threw her down the stairs, down to where her mother still stood. Not satisfied, he took the stairs in leaps to the bottom, where he kicked Rita repeatedly in the back as she lay helpless on the floor. Rita's mother screamed and begged him to stop.

Nina watched at first and then she fled to the house next door. The neighbour rushed over to intervene. Another neighbour took Rita to the hospital. Her stepfather was arrested and found guilty of assault. He spent six months in jail, and part of his release agreement was that he would not touch Rita ever again. Rita maintained throughout her life that it was this beating, rather than her polio, that prevented her from walking.

Just weeks after her stepfather was released from jail, Rita was returning home from school. It was slow going, as usual, on her crutches. As she neared the house, she heard screaming. It was her mother's voice. Rita moved as fast as she could, but found the door locked when she arrived. The screaming continued and finally she battered through the window pane of the door with one of her crutches. Her stepfather came towards the door, and, through the window, Rita delivered a blow to his head with one of her crutches. He staggered backwards and a butcher's knife clattered out of his fist onto the floor. Rita's mother was at the door in a shot and opened it. The stepfather retreated, stunned, still bleeding from the impact of the crutch Rita had levelled on him.

After this incident, Rita and Nina did everything they could to convince their mother to leave, but she never would. She was a Free Methodist and divorce was a sin. "I married him," she said sadly to them. "I have to live with my decision."

"That's your choice, Mother," said Rita. "But I won't live here anymore."

Rita was nothing if not strong-willed, no matter what her age or circumstances. The reality, though, was that she was thirteen years old. Her sister was twelve. They had polio. Their stepfather was an abusive alcoholic. Their mother felt she could no longer care for them properly. She couldn't stomach the violence either, but obviously didn't have it in her to leave her husband. Rita told Colleen Swenson, who once worked with Rita, that her mother felt her stepfather would kill the girls if they stayed. And so she put them on a train from Minneapolis to Alberta.

We no longer have Rita or Nina to tell us what that must have felt like, but it's only too easy to imagine the heartbreak. The train pulling out of the station, their mother standing on the platform, the two girls with their noses pressed to the window waving goodbye. They were on a train ride to more than fifty years of confinement. Rita and Nina were met at the border by a Canadian social worker who escorted them the rest of the way to Michener Centre, an institution for "mental defectives," located in Red Deer, Alberta.

There are different stories and different memories. Rita has told some people that her mother wrote a letter to Canada asking where a young girl on crutches could live. But Rita has also told people over the years that her stepfather forced her mother to send them away, and that she told the girls they were going to live with an aunt and an uncle back home in Alberta.

Rita and Nina believed they were to meet relatives back in Alberta. Why wouldn't they? They even continued to think it was going to happen long after they'd been placed in Michener Centre. Rita once wrote in a newsletter for the Alberta Association for Community Living (AACL) that her mother may have even actually believed she was sending them to relatives, but that when the girls arrived, the relatives changed their minds. Whatever the truth of it, the result was the same. Two bright and intelligent young girls were locked away for the next half-century. Once at Michener Centre, Nina was found to have a mild learning disability, and was placed in the "retarded" ward of Michener. The two sisters were separated.

Rita remembered those years with the kind of passion and rage that only gross injustice can keep stoked. She was regularly forced to scrub floors even though she required crutches to stand. She had to clean the diapers of incontinent adults. She cleaned feces off the walls of the rubber-celled detention rooms. It was an endless series of demeaning and disgusting jobs. She rarely slept well, because she was housed in a chaotic dorm of "mental patients." The food, she once said, "was so bad I wouldn't feed it to a dog. And I didn't even always get fed, depending on how much of a fuss I was kicking up." Year after year of this daily grind passed. And then she had her 21st birthday.

Twenty-one years old. A lost father, an abusive stepfather, abandonment by her mother, confinement, endless humiliation and a lifetime of the same to look forward to. Hardly the blossoming of a young woman's life. Not long after her birthday, she mustered up the courage to approach a staff person.

"When am I going to get out of here?" she asked.

"Never," said the staff person. "You're a retard."

Rita made the hardest decision she'd ever made. She thought first of Nina, but couldn't help herself. It was too much. She thought, "I've asked them to let me out of here for the last time."

She made her way to the highest window she could find and forced it open, pushing the screen out, and breaking the glass in the process. It was the middle of the day. She took a shard of the glass and slit her wrists with it. Then she swung her legs out over the sill and wiggled herself to a position where she could fall to the courtyard below, a drop high enough to kill her. But as she tried to summon the courage to fling herself over, a man doing some painting in the courtyard saw her and ran off for help. They got to Rita in time, and the staff pulled her from the edge.

There were no thank-yous or tearful post-rescue hugs. No sitting down for a long talk and some counselling. They put her into a cell which was empty except for a toilet, first roughly pulling her arms back and tying them. Her bed was a strip of canvas on the floor. They shut the door, and she remained in that cubicle for the next six months. There was one window, high up, hard against the ceiling so that she couldn't get to it, or see out of it.

"For those six months," she once told her friend Rosie, "I

lived like an animal." When mealtime came around, a small trapdoor near the floor was opened and a tin plate of food would appear, liquids slopping all over solids.

"After those six months," Rita said. "They moved me to another hospital (Alberta Hospital in Ponoka) for electric shock treatments. The first time they connected electrodes to my head and shot current into my skull, I was scared speechless. This went on every day for four years. I was told it was to make me forget the past. By then I wouldn't have cared if they'd thrown me into the garbage dump. I no longer felt human. For seven years I was there, before being sent back to Red Deer. Once, during those black years my mother came to see me. I looked at her out of glazed eyes and spat, 'She's not my mother!' Her heart was broken and she left. I never saw her again."

Rita and Nina never did see their mother again. Yet, decades later, Rita told Colleen Swenson that she'd forgiven her mother "a long time ago."

There were further disgraces. Rita never had a sexual relationship in her life, and yet she died not even knowing if she was a virgin. She remembered waking up many times to find male orderlies in bed with her. Whatever might have happened to her through those decades at the Michener Centre, she was either too drugged to remember or she simply forced it from her mind. The drugs may have also affected her dream life. She had a recurring dream while in Alberta Hospital about waking up in bed to see a nurse with a horse's head standing over her. "It was all so real, though I was so drugged up."

There is the possibility that she was sterilized while at Michener, though she has said that she refused the procedure when she went before the Eugenics Board, the provincial authority responsible for the sterilization of persons it deemed to be mentally defective. (Though this abhorrent practice was eradicated in 1972, there are lawsuits pending against the government for wrongful sterilization.) We do know, however, that Rita had surgeries at various times without knowing what they were for. She once told Colleen, "What would I have to offer a man in a relationship? Nothing." She was afraid of men for years after she left the institution, and only gradually attained a comfort level that allowed male staff to work with her.

Through all the treatments at Alberta Hospital, Rita realized one thing – she wasn't going to get out. Resisting would only intensify her punishment. She would be assigned tasks such as being given a toothbrush to clean feces off the rubber-walled detention room. "But they never broke me," Rita once said. "I realized that screaming and fighting only made them drug me and shock me more. So I never said anything. But inside I was screaming."

&

Rita and Nina had rarely seen one another during the seven years Rita was at Alberta Hospital. While we know little about Rita during these years, we know even less about Nina. Unlike Rita, Nina would not talk about her life. She would say simply that it was "too sad" to think about.

Things had, however, actually begun to change slightly at Michener Centre during Rita's absence. A new social worker had come on the scene, a Scotsman, Rita remembers, and he'd begun trying to institute change to the antiquated Michener treatment practices. He asked every one of his patients, "Would you like to leave and go back to your family?" Most looked at him with disinterest or incomprehension. Not Rita. She spoke immediately and surely. "Can I leave today?"

This social worker, whose name has unfortunately been lost, took a personal interest in Rita from then on, investigating options for her. Yet it still took decades. Finally, in the mid-1970s, he reported to her that a new nursing home, Dickensfield Extended Care, was being built, and though all the beds were full, they were building another wing. One day he took her to see it as it neared completion, and he asked her what she thought. "It's a palace!" she cried. Her very next thought was, I'm not leaving without Nina.

୫

In 1979, Rita and Nina moved from Michener Centre to Dickensfield, though they must have done so in a daze, disbelieving that they were actually leaving Red Deer. They had, after all, first arrived there in 1928. Both sisters were now out from under the oppressive structure of a large institution they should never have entered to begin with. Dickensfield, though not at all like Michener Centre, was still an institution and it was not what Rita truly hungered for. After a few years at Dickensfield, she moved to Bader Towers, a supported living arrangement in the community.

Nina, conversely, found her time at Dickensfield somewhat easier to handle than did Rita. She was there for eighteen years, and enjoyed the activities and the staff who assisted her with her painting. She loved to paint, and it was at Dickensfield that her talent blossomed. She continued to paint until the end of her life, working with landscapes and animal figures. One of Nina's gorgeous watercolours is the cover image for this book, and oth-

47

ers appear at the beginning of each chapter. Many of her paintings are proudly displayed in the homes of people she knew and liked. Some of her work even went on to win awards, so high was their quality.

Earl Bridges, whose wife Myrna and their family were friends of the Haggerty sisters, jokes that Nina didn't do quite as many paintings in her last few years, because, he said, "She kept complaining that it was getting too expensive to frame them all."

"I told her," says Earl, "that she didn't have to frame each and every one. I mean, she could have just given a painting to someone and let them frame it themselves, but she didn't like to give something to someone unless it was just the way she wanted it, and she wanted her paintings in frames."

Nina made many friends during her time at Dickensfield. Some of these friends went on vacation with Nina, places such as Jasper and Las Vegas, although she complained cheekily about "those machines that kept taking my money." This was why she said she'd never go back to Vegas, despite the fun she had!

Both sisters liked to take holidays. Even though they hadn't been able to travel until late in life, Rita had been to Hawaii, and had also travelled to Phoenix, Jasper, Banff, Victoria and Kananaskis. Nina had been to Disneyland, and in 1997 went on the trip of her life when she and Marilyn McNeilly, a support worker, went on an Alaskan cruise. Nina was beside herself with excitement about this trip. She loved being on a boat, the awesome scope of nature, the overwhelming beauty of the scenery. She didn't mind the attention she received from all the staff, either. They treated her like a royal visiting dignitary, and she revelled in it.

There were many people who contributed to Rita and Nina's life once they left Michener Centre. Many brought both Rita and Nina into their homes, and made them part of the family. This was certainly the case for Nina and her relationship with the Bridges family.

"Oh, she was part of the family," says Myrna, smiling. "She was at the weddings of all our children and came to family dinners all the time."

Of the many stories that Myrna and Earl can recall, one in particular still brings a laugh to their faces. At Christmas some years ago, they offered Nina a glass of wine, not thinking much of it. Nina, never having had alcohol in her life, and not really knowing even quite what it was, said yes.

"Apparently she liked the taste of it," says Earl, smiling and shaking his head. "Because she just up and gulped it down in one go. Anyway, pretty soon the room was spinning."

"And," adds Myrna, "I don't think the staff were too happy with us after. They were the ones that had to stay up all night with Nina while she was being sick."

The funniest part of the story is that for years thereafter Myrna and Earl would jokingly offer Nina a glass of wine at special occasions. "Here you go, Nina," they'd say. "You can handle this, can't you?"

"Oh no," she'd cry. "No, take that away." And they'd all burst out laughing at the memory of Nina's first and last taste of alcohol.

Rita and Nina were able to spend the last years of their lives living together first in an apartment, and then in a house, with the support of a local agency that provides residential supports to people with disabilities. How Rita and Nina came to be with that agency is in some ways a piece of good luck, not just for Rita and Nina, but for the others who got to know them and witness their spirit.

In 1994, Rita, who was a powerful and committed speaker, was at a conference on aging, talking about her life and the hardships she had survived. Wendy Hollo was there to hear Rita tell her tale. She returned to the agency and immediately suggested they offer service to Rita. Bev Hills, a Program Manager with the agency, followed up, working with Alberta Association for Community Living (AACL) to get Rita and Nina approved for the funding that would allow them to live in their own home. The AACL provided essential financial support.

Even with this direct intervention, it still took a dramatic event to get Rita to this agency. She'd been living in Bader Towers for twelve years, but had then broken her leg. Bader was unable to continue to care for her because they didn't have the staff required to care for someone with Rita's intense physical care needs. She also contracted pneumonia at this time, and so was finally moved to St. Joseph's Extended Care, where she remained for a year and a half. It was only after her stay at St. Joseph's that she was able to move to the agency.

While Rita was at St. Joseph's, Nina began to think about the possibility of leaving Dickensfield to live in the community. She was apprehensive, as she had a right to be, after so many decades in institutions. However, she had the courage to try, so in September of that year she moved into her own apartment in the west end of the city, right across the hallway from Rita, now home from St. Joseph's. She and Rita shared staff supports. This was one of the proudest moments not only of Nina's life, but of Rita's, too. She had always said that she would never leave Michener without her sister. She'd achieved that, and now here they were, living like real people across the hall from one another in the community, with no one telling them what to do every second of the day. This may seem so ordinary to those of us who take it for granted, but it was a monumental day for these two sisters. They were now free as members of the community, a position they'd not been in together since they were little girls, seven decades earlier.

"Rita was so excited about every little thing," remembers Myrna Bridges. "She used to call me up to say she'd made muffins. She was so excited by that. She'd used tin foil cups, real blueberries. All done in the oven. She was just thrilled."

There were other small domestic pleasures that Rita delighted in. Christmas became one of her favourite times of the year. She enjoyed decorating the house, doing the tree up just right. Of course, true to her imperious style, she generally sat in her wheelchair giving out orders to everybody else as to exactly how it ought to be done. She loved her home, and loved the fact that she lived in the community.

Nina had also approached the move very positively, though she had made such strong friends at Dickensfield who she missed greatly after moving out. Visits back and forth were frequent. After eighteen months of apartment living, the two women decided (*they* decided!) that they would prefer to live in a house, a place where they'd have a little more privacy and a deck out back. The house they found was central and they had to spend less time on the Disabled Adults Transit System (DATS) bus. In May of 1997, they moved out of the apartment building and into a house together, free under one roof for the first time in seventy years.

Now that she was living in the community, Nina finally had a little bit of money to spend. The staff helped her budget and to learn to save money, skills that people in institutions usually do not learn. This is what allowed her to have a vacation, to buy a new bedroom suite. "She literally had no clothes when she came to us," said Marilyn McNeilly. "Nothing. But she so loved having the freedom to actually go out and buy something. One of the first things she bought herself was a ring. She was so excited by this, that she got to buy herself a ring." Rita didn't mind spending a little money, either. She loved to unload a few dollars here and there, and wasn't going to let her sister do all the spending.

This was the house they remained in until each passed away, Rita just before Christmas 1998 and Nina shortly thereafter. There is little doubt that the last few years of their lives were the happiest, most free and most fulfilling. They died knowing they achieved something, not just for themselves, but for all those who fight for the same thing, the right to live independently.

ॐ

Nina and Rita were women of great faith, though it was certainly sorely tested in their early lives. This faith was a strong component of their characters, and it really began to take shape in their years at Dickensfield. Rita's prayers at Michener Centre had gone so completely unanswered for decades that she often challenged God by looking into the skies and shouting, "You don't exist!" Still, Rita's life was not without interventions, divine or otherwise.

Both Rita and Nina were members of the Apostolic Church in south Edmonton. They joined the church through the urgings of a friend Rita made while at Dickensfield, Agnes Mentz, who was a member of the church and encouraged Rita to come along and try it out. She did and loved it.

Annette Sabo has been a long-time member of the Apostolic congregation, and she remembers how much the church meant to both women. "I think you could say that it was kind of like a family for them. A family they never really had at all, up until they joined our church, and until they moved into their supported home. They had two families that meant so much to them."

It was at the Apostolic Church that Rita also started to learn to read again, something that had been denied her for the previous sixty years. JoAnn Sabo, Annette's sister-in-law, remembers how much joy Rita got from learning phonetically, using the very same materials the grade school kids used.

Both Nina and Rita were baptized in the Apostolic Church. "That was a first for our church," says JoAnn, chuckling a little at the memory of it. "Baptizing Rita in a wheelchair. And it was a full immersion, too. The wheelchair and everything. Right under."

Nina loved to sing hymns at the Church. Brother Cal, then the Pastor at the Apostolic Church, once shouted out at a service that Jesus loved us all, and then asked the congregation,

"How do we know that?" Quick as a whip, Nina responded, "Because the Bible tells us so." Church services and activities were a central part of Nina's life and she went as often as she could right up to her last days. Both women attended the Apostolic Church for many years, and found there a sense of acceptance and family they had had so little of in their lives. It must have felt so new to them the first time they experienced it.

"Rita used to enjoy going to church so much," says Colleen Swenson, "that sometimes she hardly slept the night before. And she loved to get nicely dressed for it. She was a bit old-fashioned in some ways, and she usually liked to wear a hat or a bow. I remember one time she couldn't find the right hat to go with what she was wearing, and suddenly she just grabbed a doily off the coffee table and slapped it on her head. 'How does that look?' she said. Well, off she went and when she came back she said how many people had told her she looked nice that day. She wore doilies on her head a lot after that."

⧉

Marilyn McNeilly once said of Nina that, "We are better people" for having known her and that she herself felt privileged to have been a part of Nina's life because "she brought a ray of sunshine into the lives of those who worked with her and those who were her friends." Certainly, calling Nina a ray of sunshine must bring a smile to the face of all those who knew both sisters, since it automatically calls to mind the somewhat different personality of Rita who had, shall we say, a slightly less sunny temperament.

Colleen Swenson recalls that Rita generally liked to "test" the staff the first few times they worked with her. "Oh, she could sound tough, that's for sure," laughs Colleen. "The first time I went into her apartment she looked me up and down and said 'Who are you?' After I passed the test, we had a great friendship, but you always had to gain that trust with Rita first. If she didn't like you, look out! She just seemed to have a great intuition about people, and if she smelled a bad attitude or any sort of patronizing attitude towards her, she would dismiss them immediately. There were rarely second chances with Rita. Of course, if she decided she liked you, she would forgive you anything."

Edith White, who was a long-time friend of Rita's, echoes this. "That was the thing about Rita. She could be difficult sometimes, for sure, but when you had her love, it was unconditional."

For all the inspiration and love they created around them, Rita and Nina did have their idiosyncracies. Marilyn, grinning, remembers that Nina "had the staff wound around her little finger." She wanted attention and she got it, says Marilyn, "You just couldn't say no to her. Rita fought to be a little more independent in the day-to-day stuff, but with Nina you couldn't say no if she asked for something."

Rita and Nina were both also well known for suggesting an activity or outing with a friend that had a hidden agenda buried in it. Their friends will laugh as they remember this trait. "Rita would call up," says Myrna, "to see if we wanted to do something, and it always turned out that she had some errand or other that we could, you know, just help her out with if we had the time. They were very smart ladies that way. Rita always had a goal, was always thinking about getting things done."

Nina was a year younger than Rita, and, says Myrna

Bridges, was "supposedly the slower of the two sisters, but if she was retarded, well, then, I should be so retarded. She was so quick-witted. She picked up on Earl's old one-liners quicker than anyone else around the table."

Nina had certainly absorbed the horror of the fights between her sister, mother and stepfather and, in Rita's opinion, she must have suffered greatly. Rita always felt it was her duty to care for her sister throughout their lives together.

"Oh, yes," says Myrna Bridges. "Rita always talked about how she wanted to get out of Michener Centre and then Dickensfield, but that she wasn't going to go unless Nina was coming with her. Probably the proudest moment of her life was when they were both out in the community. She said to me, 'I did it, I got us out.' She was so happy. Only it took seven decades."

Rita and Nina were each other's family. In 1980, when their mother passed away, they found out about it only through a letter forwarded by the lawyer handling their mother's estate. There was a half-brother from her mother's second marriage, but his existence is lost. There are no other relatives known.

Still, they had so much capacity for love and joy, and took pleasure from little things. "Rita loved flowers," says Colleen Swenson. "We'd be walking along somewhere, and she was always commanding me to pick her some flowers. 'Oh, Colleen,' she'd say, 'just reach up and pick those lilacs, come on, Colleen, reach, reach, come on, get up on that fence and pick me those lilacs.' You couldn't say no. She had such a good sense of humour about things, despite everything. Just witnessing Rita's and Nina's struggle changed my life. They gave me humility, and always left me in complete awe with their faith and perseverance despite all the obstacles."

Marilyn McNeilly was beside each woman during their last hours, and she performed the eulogies for both. "Nina's was somehow more difficult to do," she says. "Probably because she was just a bit less independent than Rita, and that made her a little more needy emotionally. A person would give her affection and attention and she would always take it. But you just can't help wondering how their lives would have turned out, what could have been," says Marilyn, emotion clogging her voice. "We can only imagine how different their lives would have been, how much fuller and better, if they'd had things go just a little bit differently. Instead, they spent seventy years in institutions because they had polio."

Marilyn says that when Rita passed away, there was finally a kind of peace displayed across her face. She'd fought all her life, and didn't have to fight anymore. Rita and Nina are now certainly together again, as they always have been and always will be. There was so much sadness to their lives, but whatever and wherever that place is that we call Heaven, Rita and Nina are there. And you can be sure they're getting it all arranged exactly to their liking. Would an angel dare stand in their way?

The days of Michener Centre, those decades of pointless life-killing boredom and degradation, were long and dark; an endless tunnel it must have seemed they'd never emerge from. Yet though they are rare, moments from that cave of darkness sometimes do suddenly find illumination, and are put under the light to remind us that human lives were behind those walls. The day before Nina's funeral service, at the viewing, a woman approached Marilyn.

"Excuse me," she said. "I just wanted to tell you that I knew

Nina at Michener Centre. I was there as a small child and spent quite a few years there. I just wanted to say that I remember Nina washing me and changing my diaper, and taking care of me as I grew. She used to braid my hair for me. I never forgot it. I never forgot her, and when I saw her obituary in the paper, I just had to come. She was so good to me, and so gentle."

Marilyn was overcome with emotion. The other staff felt tears come to their eyes. Nina had often talked about how she'd looked after babies and children at Michener Centre, but no one ever knew how much credence to place in the stories, or even how much the stories were just Nina's own wish that she'd had someone who'd done that for her in her own childhood. And now here was proof. A person no one had ever heard of appearing at Nina's memorial tribute to say how thankful she was for Nina's presence in her life, and to say, above all else, that she remembered.

After she spoke to Marilyn, however, the woman left quietly, without leaving her name or where she could be reached. In a lifetime of losses for Rita and Nina Haggerty, it was yet another disappearance. The woman was gone.

Rita Haggerty

Victoria, Photo by M. McNeilly

Nina Haggerty

Alaskan Cruise, 1998

The Flower

The Happiest Guy on the Planet

To say that Davie Suru has a sunny disposition is more than just a comment on his outlook. He has a sunny out-look…literally. Sometimes, it's a tornado outlook. Or a cyclone outlook. Maybe a hurricane, depending on his luck. The man loves the weather. Sitting at the dining room table of the house he shares with his good friend David, I decide to test his clear-ly prodigious weather knowledge.

"Okay, look outside."

He looks.

"What kind of clouds are those?"

"Oh," he laughs, giggling like Einstein being asked two plus two. "Stratocumulus. Anybody knows that."

"Oh…right," I say. "Who wouldn't."

"I want to be a storm chaser," says Davie. He'd be great at it, that's for certain. One thing Davie can never get enough of is weather. He's a weather nut. Storms, tornadoes, hail, gales, cyclones. One thing he doesn't like for some reason, are floods. How come? "Because people die in floods," he says, eyes wide. I didn't quite have the heart to tell him that people die in tornadoes, too. And cyclones. And hurricanes.

Davie loves the weather so much he once made an appearance on the weather segment of ITV News, or at least a device of his making did. One evening in the spring of 1999, Claire Martin, a popular Edmonton weather announcer, told her audience that she was going to demonstrate the physical properties of a tornado using two 2-litre pop bottles, 1 litre of liquid, a balloon and some duct tape. She also told her audience that this contraption was the work of one Davie Suru, loyal weather watcher. She proceeded to demonstrate Davie's home funnel machine, in which the pop bottles are aligned mouth-to-mouth, then ballooned and taped together to create a seal, with one of the bottles almost full. Claire then gave the contraption a couple of quick swirls to create a whirlpool from one bottle to the other, holding them upright. Bingo, a recreation of a tornado. The first time Davie demonstrated it for me, I was transfixed. I looked over at Davie and Jerry Campbell, who worked with Davie for four years. My face must have said it all. Davie was grinning.

"I know," said Jerry, who was also grinning. "Isn't that the coolest thing you've ever seen?"

"You must have been proud to have had this thing on TV." I said to Davie. He grins and gives his trademark utterance. "Of course!"

Davie was born in Stettler, Alberta in 1969, one of twins. His twin sister, Lori Hansen, lives in Onoway and has children of her own. At birth, Davie was diagnosed with Down's Syndrome, and was placed in an incubator for two weeks. When he was two months old, a doctor told his parents he would be completely dependent, and that he would never walk, talk, or be able to feed himself and that he'd likely be dead by the age of sixteen. The implication was that he ought to be institutionalized. To look at Davie today – at his sheer vibrancy, his joys, his athletic accomplishments – is to be horrified that perhaps many other babies like Davie were assigned to institutions and ended up living lives that were grotesquely unrealized. To Davie's great good fortune, his parents were strong enough to say "No, we don't believe that." Davie went home with his parents, and was from the start an accepted part of the family, living in the family home.

"I remember it so clearly," says Louise Suru, Davie's mother. "They told me straight to my face all that stuff about never walking, talking, being able to feed himself. It was a pediatrician from Edmonton. That doctor is still working today. I've often thought I ought to take Davie over there." How instructive that would be, how satisfying, though we know it's satisfaction enough simply to have Davie here as he is today.

Lynda Bykewich has been a friend of Louise Suru's since long before Davie was born, and she remembers Davie well as a child. "He was just as happy then as he is now," she laughs. "And even as a kid you could tell that when he laughed it came right from his toes."

Lynda thinks that Davie's demeanor, his manners and good nature are the direct result of his mother Louise being the person she is. When people would say to her that Davie would never be able to do this or that, she'd say, "Wrong! She never ever treated him differently that his twin sister, Lori. They were disciplined the same way and treated the same way."

Louise agrees. "One huge advantage that I think Davie did have growing up," says Louise, "was that he had a twin in Lori. Because whatever it was she did, he would try it. They were exceptionally close growing up. It wasn't even until they were twelve that they had their first fight."

Davie began attending school at Winnifred Stewart School, a school specifically for persons with mental disabilities, when he was three and he remained there until the age of twelve. Following his completion of the programs at Winnifred Stewart, he went on to Junior High School at H.E. Beriault, where he earned his Junior High Diploma when he was sixteen. He then went to Austin O'Brien, where he earned his High School Diploma. Both Beriault and O'Brien are schools with general student populations. Davie attended mainstream classes and had an aide working with him.

However not all was smooth for Davie as he progressed through his school years. Moving from the protected environment of Winnifred Stewart to the regular school environment of H.E. Beriault did cause Louise some concern. "That was mostly our own worry," says Louise. "We were worried. Still, he could do everything they had for him at Winnifred Stewart, and we had to let him try to learn along with the others at Beriault. As it turned out, it wasn't a problem at all. He didn't have any problems at all integrating, or learning, or getting along."

The transition from Beriault to Austin O'Brien was good, but had its own set of worries, just because the school was so much bigger. And there was the issue of the bus. He took the school bus until his teachers decided he could handle the Edmonton Transit Service bus. They trained him well, but, says Louise, "I was a nervous wreck!"

Still, Davie took the Edmonton Transit Service bus by himself every day to and from school. "Which is amazing," says Louise, "because usually he falls asleep on the bus." Louise recounts the story of how Davie did in fact once fall asleep on the bus coming home from Austin O'Brien. He missed his stop, and ended up downtown. Louise was frantic and had all the neighbours out scouring the streets for him. As it turned out, Davie struck up a conversation with one of the drivers downtown, who helped him get back as far as the mall. At this point the driver made the incredible decision, at night in the middle of an Edmonton winter, to then let Davie walk home from there, without telling anybody they'd even found him. Fortunately, as Davie was about halfway home, one of the neighbours found him.

⅋

One cold day in January, I visited Davie at his home near Meadowlark Mall. After Davie and I got settled and started in on a conversation, David, his roommate, interrupted us.

"Excuse me," said David politely but firmly. "Excuse me, but can I just say one thing here?"

We looked over at David.

"Really, Davie," said David, wagging a finger. "Should you

just be wearing a t-shirt in here? I mean, it's cold outside. Are you warm enough?"

Davie waves a dismissive hand at David. "Aww, just ignore that guy," he laughs.

"OK," says David, holding up both hands in the air. "That's all I'm saying."

Davie and David have been friends forever, it seems. They met through Special Olympics. It was during his time at Winnifred Stewart School that Davie began his long involvement with Special Olympics. It has been a long and fruitful relationship. That's one way to put it. The other way is to just call it like it is… Davie's a jock. He's got that instinctive athletic posture, coupled with the ability to take a simple pure pleasure in performing complicated physical actions. He has that ease and confidence in his body most true athletes possess, which makes the pediatrician's statements that he'd never walk or talk all the more staggering.

"His technique with most sports has always been excellent," says Louise. Indeed, Davie is a great student of form and function, and he understands athletic movement. "He's not all that fast," says Louise. "But his technique, at almost everything he does, is excellent, and he learns so well."

There are so many sports Davie enjoys and does well. One sport in which he has real potential is powerlifting. Another that he loves is track and field, a sport in which his mother coaches both him and other athletes. Louise has been involved with the Special Olympics for 20 years and is now the chairperson of the Edmonton branch. Davie is one of 70 Edmonton area athletes competing in track and field.

In Special Olympics, athletes can enter five events at track and field tournaments, one of which must be a field event. While Davie loves track and field, it's not the sport in which he's going to maximize his athletic potential. As for his swimming, he does the backstroke, the breaststroke, the sidestroke, the butterfly and freestyle. "He has amazing endurance," marvels Jerry. "If they had swimming endurance events, he'd win every one." Davie's sister Lori was his swim coach until she moved to Onoway. He's been involved in the Nationals in swimming, as well as soccer, which has lead Jerry to describe Davie, lovingly, as a "real fitness freak."

"Of course!" says Davie. "I love to work out!" And his favourite drink is water, water, water, just like every high-calibre athlete.

If there is one sport in which Davie might truly have superb potential it is figure skating. He actually started out in speed skating, but while he could easily match the other competitors for form, he couldn't keep up in speed. At one of his first events, held in Red Deer, Alberta, he came over to the side of the rink after one race and said to his mother, "Can you tell those other guys to slow down so that I can catch up?" It was his inability to match power with technique that led to the move to figure skating.

Sarah Lavin has been teaching Davie figure skating for over eight years now, and she remembers that Davie's mom encouraged the move. "Oh, yeah, she was right behind it," says Sarah. "We all could see that Davie is just so dramatic with his movements and he's such a showman. Figure skating is a perfect fit for him."

Sarah notes that Davie has made tremendous advances in his technique in the last few years. "He has great courage. He's not afraid to fail, and he's not afraid to fall, either," she laughs. There are so many positive advantages to figure skating for Davie, says Sarah. Not only is it a great athletic pursuit, one in which he has genuine talent, but there's a great social atmosphere to it, and a competitive one, if you want it. It also encourages sportsmanship.

Davie can do beautiful spirals on both feet, though sometimes he gets nervous. He competed the very first year he came over to figure skating, and has now gone so far as to compete in the Provincial championships. He and Sarah define success for him not so much by outcomes but by process and by personal goals. The day I went to watch Davie practice, it happened to be Beach Day, and he was wearing a tie-dyed shirt and a floppy beach hat. "He loves to dance," laughs Sarah. "He loves music and rhythm. He's a great actor and he's so charming."

"He's got great potential in figure skating," says Louise. "He usually gets top marks for dance and for the way he skates to the music. It's one sport he could genuinely be at a top level." Davie may have found his true niche. Louise tells the story of last year's figure skating Special Olympics. Davie finished his routine, and afterwards they handed out flowers, a standard practice. Never one to miss an opportunity, Davie took one of the flowers, placed it squarely between his teeth, and began bowing to the adoring crowd.

৪৩

Davie has recently turned thirty, but to look at his boyish handsomeness and enthusiasm for life, you might think he was seventeen. "Oh yeah," says Jerry, a staff person. "You will simply never ever meet a happier guy than Davie."

Davie is funny, has a great sense of humour, and he's very giving, physically and emotionally. He's also a very honest person, and will always support his peers. Louise remembers the time Davie was competing in a track event. He was ahead of a friend coming around the turn of the track, but she tripped and fell. Davie stopped racing, and went back to help her up. He's good at encouraging people around him to try things.

One thing Davie will always encourage others to do is to sing, though that generally means listening to him, too! Davie loves singing, loves music, loves dancing. He's got a karaoke machine in the basement and he loves singing so much that he's taken many of his favourite songs and actually transcribed the words into a binder he keeps on a music stand, so that he can put on the earphones, plug in the karaoke machine and let 'er rip. He thinks he sounds great, but then, so do we all. His sense of rhythm and timing is excellent. He knows the words to some songs so well that he doesn't even need his song sheets.

ⅎ

Paid work is something that is a focus for Davie these days. Sports are great, but he can't figure skate all day. "I'd say that's a pretty important thing right now," says Louise. "Finding him a job that has meaning and that actually pays him for that work."

Davie has had good jobs in the past, the best of which was working in the kitchen at the restaurant On 40th in southwest Edmonton. The owner was a progressive employer who treated his staff with disabilities the same as any other staff, and paid them properly. Unfortunately, On 40th overextended the number of staff it needed and Davie was laid off from that job. Davie experienced the opposite at his job with a large pizza chain. He worked there for three months, while his employer got a government subsidy to pay Davie a wage. At the end of the three months, the employer told Davie his work was excellent and that he could keep working but would only be paid in pizza for lunch. Louise told him he could take his ham and mushroom and bake it.

For many years, Davie has held a volunteer position at the Misericordia Hospital doing the mail and helping nurses put together their charts. Louise job-shadowed him once. "I couldn't believe how complicated it was." He's been a model volunteer, and has won many awards for both hours and service. He's also currently working at the Jamie Platz YMCA, where he helped out in the daycare washing dishes and cleaning tables, and is now working in the fitness area. He cleans the fitness machines and loves it because he is so close to all the athletic equipment he uses for his chest and biceps workouts. You can tell he uses the machines as well as cleans them just by looking at his arms. Don't arm wrestle him for dish duty or you'll end up with dishpan hands.

ം

At home, Davie loves to take people on tours. He'll show you his stacks of weather books. In his bedroom, he'll show you some of his prized possessions, and then he'll stop and grin and point at the ceiling. You look up, and there are a constellation of stars glued tight and shiny. He'll take you through the kitchen. Davie likes to cook, but loves to eat even more, and, says Lynda, "his favourite meal is always the one you've just made." He also seems to believe that you can eat anything you want as long as you eat jello afterwards to prevent weight gain.

In the living room, he'll point to his video collection. Unsurprisingly, *Twister* is present and accounted for, but charmingly, so are multiple reruns of *I Love Lucy*.

"Oh, I think those are so funny," he laughs. "Especially the one where she sits at the bottom of the shower and it fills up." He giggles and makes the rest of us laugh, too, until someone goodnaturedly brings up a small incident at the last place he lived. "Oh, yeah," says Davie, "Oops. I sat in the shower like Lucy and tried to fill it up. The tub overflowed." He turns and looks at Jerry, giving him a serious look. "We need to get the shower door sealed on that better so the water won't leak out."

"Right," says Jerry, with somewhat more skepticism than optimism.

Davie does like his movies, particularly the scary ones. His favourites are *Nightmare on Elm Street, Night of the Demons* and *Midnight Hour.* He likes old funny movies, animated movies. *Curly Sue* was a favourite. His sister Lori sometimes gets scared at movies. She once spilt her popcorn while watching *Nightmare on Elm Street* with Davie. "I love my sister," he grins. "But she gets scared at scary movies."

Davie's sister is not the only relative he gets on well with. He is great with his sister's kids and wants to teach his niece, Niki, to skate. And he loves his two aunts, Auntie Pie Face and Auntie Giggles. One is named for an infamous family pie fight in which both Aunt Vickie and Davie emerged covered in pie. The other is named for the fact that whenever Davie and Aunt Norma get together, they reduce each other to fits of laughing. Whenever Davie sees Auntie Pie Face now, he suggests a pie fight. Every time. And whenever he sees Auntie Giggles, he starts to laugh before she even says a word, then she starts to laugh, and pretty soon, they're both in tears of laughter and not a word's been spoken.

℘

Davie has been living in the community for three years now with the help of a local agency offering residential support services. It was a transition that Louise admits was not made easily. "I just thought, he's so comfortable at home, but what if something happens to me, what then? Not that he couldn't adjust. He would. But it would take him a while. And so why not do it now, when everyone's around to help and support the transition. And it has gone great."

The people who work with Davie agree. "He's just a great guy to be around," laughs Jerry. "He's always willing to help out around the house. He likes his TV just like the rest of us, but he can be incredibly motivated, too." The only real moments of unease for Davie in the community tend to come during times of high stress. Davie can get scared when someone around him is expressing great anger, or if he thinks his well-being is under threat. He can even get scared sometimes by arguments in the house.

Which is not to say that Davie doesn't enjoy a good time. "I like to drink beer," laughs Davie, who can put it away at the rate of about half a bottle every four hours. "I like a good party, too." A group from the agency has a dance once a month and Davie participates in those regularly.

Community living can sometimes be worrisome for those people around Davie, who know that he is trusting to a fault. Louise won't let Davie go to the mall on his own – not because he can't get there and navigate himself, but because she worries about strangers. Davie knows not to talk to strangers, but if he happens to start talking to someone and likes them, they aren't strangers anymore. He'd lend them his bank card, tell them his PIN number and help them spend the cash.

"Still," says Lynda, who has known him as long as anyone, "there's an incredible sense of people that he possesses. He's an uncanny judge of people. There aren't many people he doesn't like, but when he doesn't like someone, there is always a reason."

The Suru's have spent many summer days at the Bykewich cabin at Garner Lake, out towards Bonnyville, Alberta. "He loves it out there," says Lynda. "He swims, he hangs out. He just loves it there. He rides the bike around the lake, says hi to everyone, and everyone knows him."

⁍

Pat Conrad, the Manager of Volunteer Services for the agency providing Davie with staffing supports, has known Davie for about four years. Davie has helped out with many things such as large mailouts, doing labels and stuffing envelopes. "The first thing I see when I think of Davie is his smile. It's a wonderful smile. He likes people. He enjoys his relationships with people. And he really likes to be successful. That's one great thing about him. He likes to do things that help out, and he likes being good at things. He's not afraid to try stuff, which means that he gets better."

And Pat can't help but mention Davie's singing. "It's such an uninhibited natural thing," grins Pat. "That's what's so wonderful about it. I'll sometimes hear him singing along in the boardroom, if he's in there doing a job, and you can tell he just gets such pleasure out of it. That's a great gift in itself. To be able to take real pleasure in things."

Davie's singing is just one aspect of that pleasure, that ability he has to enjoy what life has given him, and to not be afraid. How is it possible, one can only think, while watching Davie skate or sing or recreate an episode of *I Love Lucy* or show you his tornado device, that there were those who suggested he'd be unable to walk or talk, that he'd be dead before the end of his teen years. Today, he is a man so willing to embrace what life has to offer that almost nothing scares him. Not even the prospect of listening to new friends sing on a karaoke machine.

"You'd let me try it?" I ask, wide-eyed.

He smiles, truly happy at the thought of sharing it with another person. "Of course!"

Davie Suru

Track and Field Tournament, 1999

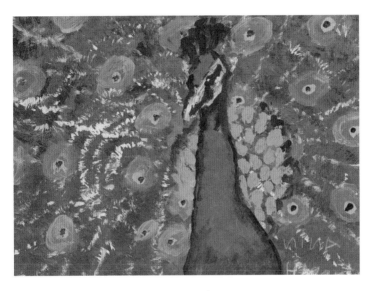

Peacock

A Complicated Life

The people who hadn't heard Karen Baum speak before were in for a treat. She did her little half-shuffle up to the stage, smiling a bit shyly as she went, fiddling with the mike when she got there. It would have been entirely reasonable to think she wasn't that comfortable with public speaking. But you'd have been wrong. She's a natural, and like every natural, she knows it, too. "How does this thing work," she half-mumbled into the microphone, smiling at the crowd as she was getting started. People were smiling along with her. She already had the crowd on her side.

It was the SKILLS Annual General Meeting held in June of 1999. Karen had gone up to the stage with Cam Petty, a facilitator with the Consumer Rights Group Karen is a big part of. Karen and Cam had been called upon to tell the gathered crowd about their experiences in Windsor, Ontario, earlier that year at the annual conference for the Ontario Association for Community Living (OACL). Cam spoke about how well Karen had handled a variety of situations. Karen, who never met a microphone she didn't like, then informed the crowd that she'd had a great time with Cam, and that it all went smoothly in Windsor, especially considering that, in the interests of frugality, she and Cam had shared a suite in the hotel. With the crowd in the palm of her hands, Karen paused, grinned, and said, "Oh, and by the way…I just want everyone to know that Cam…was a perfect gentleman."

The crowd, already enjoying the talk, erupted with laughter, as did Cam. They returned to their seats amidst applause. Later, I asked Karen about the remark, and told her how funny I thought it was, that her comic timing was perfect.

"Well, not really," she said, grinning impishly, her eyes twinkling behind her glasses. "I just wanted everybody to know that Cam was a gentleman, that's all."

଼ଉ

Karen was born in 1956 in Grande Prairie, Alberta. She's the third of four children. Jean and Joan, her older sisters, are twins. Jean lives in St. Albert and Joan lives in Medicine Hat. Curtis is their younger brother. He lives in Edmonton, in the family home where he, Karen and their siblings lived after the family moved from Grande Prairie to Edmonton in 1968.

Karen was not born with a disability. She suffered a serious case of pneumonia as a child. Her sister Jean is unsure how old Karen was, but Curtis seems to remember that she was around five years old when she became ill. Karen herself is pretty sure she was three. She contracted an extremely high fever through this pneumonia, and they were unable to get her temperature down. Curtis says that her temperature was well over 105 degrees.

Nobody in the family was aware that there had even been any permanent effects from this illness until a couple of years later when Karen began attending school in Grande Prairie. It then became clear she was suffering from some sort of cognitive deficit. Why, the family asked themselves. After consulting with doctors, and reviewing her history of illnesses, they decided that it must have been the excessive fever that caused the damage. It showed up in her reading and spelling. She was falling behind the other children, even at that early age.

"It's so hard to see these things when kids aren't in school," says Jean. "Kids always develop at different rates, and Karen didn't seem any different than anyone else. She was happy and friendly and bright. I remember that she was just so totally lovable as a child." Jean pauses for a moment. "And that aspect of her certainly hasn't changed. She's an accommodating person, and she just gets along so well with everybody."

"She was always that way," says Curtis. "Even as a kid, she was always a lot of fun. She was never withdrawn or anything like that. She played with dolls, did all the regular things. I mean, she was just like any other kid."

Jean recalls that around the house Karen was also treated as an equal with her brothers and sisters, and that she had a tremendous amount of respect for her Mother and Father. She'd managed to get through the first couple of grades in Grande Prairie, but then the intellectual disability began to interfere.

"I'm not sure exactly how much we knew about her condition in Grande Prairie," says Jean, "but it wasn't until we moved to Edmonton that it became obvious."

Karen's memory of how her disability became apparent is typically colourful and unique. "I remember we were kids, and Curtis and I were playing in the snow. We made a snow fort. This was up in Grande Prairie. I climbed on top of it to test it out, to see how hard the roof was, and it collapsed and I fell on top of Curtis." Karen stops and giggles at the memory. "I nearly killed poor Curtis. But that was when I knew something was wrong with me. I had to go get Mom to dig him out."

☙

One of Cam Petty's favourite stories about Karen is from the trip they made to the OACL conference in Windsor, the same conference at which he was such a gentleman. "That was a time when she really came through in the clutch," says Cam. "I mean, we were there supposedly just as observers, but when we got there the organizers asked us if we wouldn't mind putting on a presentation about all the work we'd been doing with the Consumer Rights Group and the Consumer Bill of Rights. We went to learn. But in the process we got asked to talk about our own experiences. And Karen was simply great at it. The formal part of things went fairly well, with us just presenting on the Consumer Bill of Rights, but it was during the Question and Answer session afterwards when Karen really took off. You should have seen her!" Roaming the room like Donahue, Karen sprinted back and forth from one side of the auditorium to the other, the cordless microphone in hand, moving to people so they could ask their questions. After they asked their questions, Karen would answer them on the spot. "She did a great job," says Cam.

Karen came into her own in many ways while in Windsor, but the trip almost turned her into a felon. During a free afternoon, she and Cam were walking around Windsor and decided to stroll through the casino. Not really paying attention (or so she cheerfully claims), Karen walked straight into one of the money counting pits. "Oh, there were freezer bags full of loonies," says Karen, grinning. "And there was this big policeman, and he told me to move right now or he'd arrest me."

"So did you move?" I ask her.

"I moved," says Karen casually, trying not to laugh. "Because by then I was finished looking."

ℬ

When she was twenty-five, Karen got a job working at the southside Army and Navy Store. She worked stocking shelves, doing odd jobs and, as she says, "keeping an eye out for shoplifters." It was also around this time that Karen began experiencing the onset of mental illness. She worked at the Army and Navy for six years, until the age of thirty-one. "It was a good place to work," she recalls. "Even though they wouldn't give me a raise."

In the end, her increasing illness played a part in her having to leave the job. She had begun accusing fellow employees of stealing from her purse. Still, she made a significant amount of money from that job. Her father helped her organize her savings, and she still lives, in part, off that money today, as well as through a trust fund set up through her parent's estate.

Karen copes well with the obstacles that arise as a result of her mental illness. She understands and recognizes the signs and manifestations of it, such as the occasional delusion, but it sometimes seems so real to her. You assure Karen, for example, that her water is not really being poisoned. She'll nod in agreement, and say, "Oh, I know it's my illness talking…but there's still someone poisoning my water."

"She's aware," says Cam. "She knows about her mental illness, but she does everything she can to be responsible about her health and her life."

Karen has received support and has an outreach worker through the agency for almost ten years now. It has been a very important time for her, and a genuine period of growth. She's become a lot more independent over that time, particularly in the last few years. Her worker now is Karen Wyrstiuk, who believes that it's primarily stress that instigates delusional episodes in Karen. "Change stresses Karen out, as does moving and boredom."

Together, the two Karens have worked on cooking, budgeting, and spend a lot of time talking about relationship and stress management. They've also been working on more than just basic skills, focussing on life management. Karen has responded well to learning new methods for coping with stress.

She's also been very active in many different organizations. She was one of Norwood Continuing Care's greatest volunteers, logging over 5000 hours of volunteer time, and earning her many volunteer awards. Karen volunteers now at the Kiwanis Lodge once a week, where she helps the seniors in a variety of activities, including facilitating the dice horse game where she and the others can lay a dollar or two on in wagers. Roy Ledger, Karen's fiancee, says that Karen's way with people is what makes her such a great volunteer. "She gives and never takes a thing. That's the way she is. She's got way more courage with things than I have," says Roy, who suffered from polio as a child, "and that's one of the things I respect so much about her."

One of the things that has helped give substantial meaning to Karen's days is the work she's done with the Consumer Rights Group. The story behind the Consumer Bill of Rights is interesting in itself, as has been Karen's involvement in it. SKILLS' Executive Director, Wendy Hollo, sat down one day a few years ago to start writing a Consumer Bill of Rights for the agency's Policy Manual. Not long into it, she thought to herself, "Wait a minute, why am I writing this?"

She contacted the noted writer and facilitator Dave Hingsburger to come to Edmonton to facilitate a process whereby a group of consumers could go about writing their own Bill of Rights, which they did. Hingsburger worked with some forty persons with disabilities, including Karen. This subsequently led to a project to put the Consumer Bill of Rights into video form, making it accessible to all those persons with disabilities who might be unable to read the written document. Karen was also heavily involved in the making of this video.

An offspring of these projects was the creation of the Consumer Rights Group (CRG). It's important to note that though the agency fully supports the CRG, there is no funding relationship. The members of the group want it that way. As Cam Petty says, they'll accept financial assistance "from anybody," but the CRG will remain a separate and freestanding organization indebted to no one but its members.

Karen's increased role in the CRG was, in many ways, spurred on by the success of both the presentation and the gathering of other information from the Windsor conference, not to mention escaping the casino without a criminal record. The

Group meets regularly, and Karen recently ran for an official role in the Group's election. She didn't gain office, but loved going through the process.

"She has enormous drive and determination," says Cam. "Nothing stops her." He sees nothing but growing leadership roles for Karen's future, and that she'll keep on adding to her contribution to society. "As opportunities for those kinds of things come up, I can easily see Karen taking them."

ଓ

Karen's parents both died in 1990. Her father was the first of her parents to become ill. He was diagnosed with bone cancer in October of 1986. He'd been a longtime manager with the Singer Sewing Machine company, and while taking night classes towards an accounting degree in the 1970s, he left Singer to work with the federal government. He earned his degree in 1977, and worked thereafter as an accountant. The cancer that had been discovered late in 1986 did go into remission to a significant enough degree that he went back to work at the end of the year.

Life remained relatively stable for the Baums from 1986-1989. Mr. Baum's cancer moved through remission and recurrence, and Karen remembers life at home fondly. "Mom and Dad were always so nice to me," she says. "And I always listened to them, and to what they had to say."

But in October of 1989, Karen's mother, who suffered from Crohn's disease, was diagnosed with an internal cancer related to the medications she was taking for the disease. Her illness moved rapidly and she passed away just months later, on the 17th of March, 1990. Karen's father had great difficulty dealing with this, and Curtis, for one, believes that was what ultimately sapped him of the strength he needed to fight his own cancer.

"I remember my Dad coming home one day early in April of 1990," recalls Curtis. "He did his taxes, then had a conversation with the family, and he basically told us that he'd lost the will to live, and that when he started to go that we weren't to use any preventive measures, just to take him to the palliative unit at the General Hospital, where Mom had been."

He died on May 14th.

One of the ways that Karen seems to have tried to cope with this loss was to find someone to love. Shortly after her father's death, she married the boyfriend she was seeing at the time. "She just ran off and got married," sighs Jean. "She phoned us up one day and said that we should all come down and meet her husband."

The marriage was not a success. "Yeah," says Karen, with absence of self-pity or self-recrimination that is so typical of her, "I think he definitely took advantage of me, financially and in other ways, too."

After less than a year, the marriage ended, though not without serious and dangerous overtones. Karen attempted suicide during this time, though she insists that she did it just to scare her then-husband, to punish him for the way he'd treated her. She ingested a large number of pills, and was hospitalized in a psychiatric ward for depression. She had also threatened him with a knife, though Karen also says that that was just a way to try and impress upon him how much he'd hurt her. Upon leaving the hospital, she moved into the supported environment of Regency Towers, an apartment complex in which people live independently but have access to in-house support services. This was where she met Roy.

"These days, her relationship with Roy is kind of her bonus points," says Curtis. "You can see the glimmer in her eyes when she talks about him."

But there are people close to Karen, family and friends, who are careful not to be too optimistic, feeling that romantic relationships have not been Karen's strong suit in the past. She has been involved in other romantic relationships over the years that were not healthy and which did not end well. On more than one occasion, the men Karen dated took advantage of her, both sexually and financially. Her sister Jean worries that there are always going to be those who might take advantage of Karen's open heart and good nature. Even Karen herself seems perfectly aware of this possibility. She'll acknowledge the potential that she might be susceptible to being taken advantage of, but it won't change her behaviour or her susceptibility to it. She's self-aware, but she yearns deeply to have people in her life that she can love and trust.

One thing that Karen has been working on with her outreach worker is gaining greater insight into the ways that relationships work, particularly her relationship with Roy. She has had such mixed success with past relationships that everyone, including Karen herself, wants to make sure that above all she is protected. Roy, for his part, says he loves Karen, plain and simple, and that he sticks with her simply because of who she is. "After all," he says. "Why would I stick around for seven years if I didn't want to? She's such a kind-hearted person, and what I really want is her love and companionship."

Roy and Karen would like to be married some day and they

refer to one another in terms of being engaged. Karen wears an engagement ring on a necklace, since the ring makes her finger swell. She's very optimistic, echoing Roy's comments. "I know he loves me," she says. "If he didn't, he wouldn't have stuck around for all these years."

೮೧

Sitting at a local Smitty's Restaurant, the empty creamers are piling up. Karen may be a "tea granny," as Curtis says, but she likes her coffee, too, and free refills are something you just don't turn down. Which means that after a few cups of coffee, there are a good dozen empty creamers littering the table. I point it out to her, and mention that maybe the waitress might think we're just drinking the cream.

Karen laughs, and then her practical side kicks in. "Nope," she says, "because this is my third cup. She'll know."

Karen has always had idiosyncrasies that she, her friends and her family can mostly laugh about. Some of these are phobias and paranoias resulting from her illness, and one of the most recurrent is that people are trying to poison her or her water supply. This led to some laughs around Jean's house a couple of years ago when Karen was staying over. The water main burst in the street out front. They were pumping in water from a hose from the neighbour's house, and there were workmen out front ripping up the street. It was all they could do to convince Karen that something wasn't going on. "It was a bad time to have someone with a water phobia staying with us," laughs Jean.

Another of Karen's idiosyncrasies is that she is somewhat, shall we say, leisurely when it comes to getting up and moving

91

and going.

"Oh, she's very slow to get moving. I remember," says Jean, laughing, "that once we all got in the car and drove away and forgot she wasn't even in the car. We looked back and there she was, running after us. It was accidental, of course. She was just in the bathroom." Jean pauses for a moment, smiles. "She did speed up after that, but, honestly, you can't put a bomb under her to get her to speed up."

Karen remembers that trip, too. "It was in Jasper," she giggles. "And I was not being that slow."

Karen Wyrstiuk has been working with Karen for over a year, and the one thing that she says sticks with her the most whenever she thinks about Karen isn't something idiosyncratic at all, but rather that Karen is "a person with a really big heart. She just does whatever she can to make you comfortable, and tries her best not to hurt anybody's feelings." Every time a visitor goes to Karen's apartment, she has tea ready and is eager to pour you a cup, get you some milk and make sure you're comfortable. She likes to entertain, and often has the Consumer Rights Group over to her apartment for various meetings. She also has Roy over every second weekend, since they alternate weekends visiting each other.

You can certainly see the light in her eye when she talks about Roy, the sparkle that Curtis first noted. But then, Karen has that look in her eyes a lot. Everybody's mother has said at one time or another, "If you don't have anything nice to say, don't say it." Karen may be the only child who ever took that completely to heart. But it's even more than saying nice things about people. She seems to always have something insightful or interesting or honest to say. If you don't pay attention, it's your loss.

Karen has the kind of outlook that allows her to reach out and support other people, no matter what her own needs may be. Cam picks Karen's dislike of flying to illustrate this for me. Karen does not particularly enjoy flying, and neither does Cam. Last year, on their way to Windsor, Karen and Cam had to make a short flight from Toronto to Windsor on a small airplane. En route, the turbulence kicked up. Karen became frightened and reached over to hold Cam's hand to steady her nerves. Unfortunately, just a few minutes after that, the turbulence got to Cam in a different way. As he was making use of his airsickness bag, the roles changed and Karen began to try to help Cam with his sickness. "It was actually amazing, once I had time to look back on it," laughs Cam. "She's such a well-rounded person that she can look for support when she needs it, but can then turn around and give out support, too, if someone needs it more than she does. She just has a great grasp of other people's realities, as well as her own."

"You just watch her go shopping at Safeway," says Karen Wyrstiuk. "She's saying hi to the elderly people that she sees. What's so wonderful about her is that she's not afraid of people. She loves people."

Karen just smiles when she hears such praise, though 'smile' is not quite a descriptive enough word. It doesn't quite capture what's behind the eyes, that sense of knowing and more importantly liking who she is. And this has always been the case no matter what difficulties and obstacles life may put in her way. "I think it's a calmness, a centredness," says Cam. "I enjoy being around her and I genuinely admire her. She's enriched my life. But it's a lot more than her accomplishments." Cam pauses for a moment. "She's just worthy of admiration, whether she's a person with a disability or not."

Karen Baum

Photo by W. Hollo, 2000

Fall

JESSIE AND EMIL KUPSCH

A Love Story

Sitting around the dinner table of their supported residence, Jessie and Emil talk with everybody, smile and laugh at jokes. They have been living as a married couple in this residence in the Westmount area of Edmonton since 1987. Jessie talks a lot more than Emil, but that's okay, because she's talking for him half the time, anyway. After one dinner, there didn't seem to be a whole lot of chicken left, even though the staff had prepared a considerable amount. Then we noticed a big pile of bones near Emil's plate.

"Boy," I said, pointing to the bones. "I think I know where all the chicken's gone."

Jessie cackles high-spiritedly. "Mabel ate it all," she laughs. Jessie has always endearingly called Emil "Mabel."

Emil, who has been bent over his plate, concentrating on his food, peers up over the rim of his big glasses. "Yeah," he says

99

smiling. He licks his lips and goes back to his plate. He's in on the joke, but there are more important things to consider, like finishing off the chicken.

Jessie reaches over and touches Emil. "Mabel likes chicken. So does Jessie."

Jean, one of the people who lives on the other side of the duplex from Jessie and Emil, is still giggling over the chicken bones. Jessie looks at her and they both keep laughing. Emil looks up good-naturedly. You can tell what he's thinking: "It is kind of funny. But boy, this chicken is good."

After dinner, we clean up. It doesn't take long with Jean loading the dishwasher, Emil wiping the table and Jessie putting the scraps and bones in the garbage.

"Come on over," says Jessie. "Come over to our side and see Mabel's office." She looks to Emil. "Is that okay, Mabel?"

Emil nods slowly and smiles. He comes with us. Jessie and Emil, who have been married almost thirteen years now, live together on one side of the duplex. Emil has a room that he uses for an office, and in it he's got a radio and tape player, a large desk, calendars and filing cabinets, all set up just right.

"This is a pretty good set up you have here, Emil," I say.

"That's right," he nods. Emil has his tapes neatly arranged so that he can get to them easily whenever he feels like listening to something. Looking through them you see mostly country music, but he's also got lots of other kinds of music – easy listening, some blues, some classics, some Disney tunes. He pulls a tape out of the case and starts it on the stereo, then he pulls something else off his desk.

"Here," Emil says, holding up a hand-made kind of scrapbook.

"Mabel makes those," says Jessie, obviously proud of Emil's handiwork.

Lately, Emil has been making notebooks, daytimers and address books from scratch. He puts them together page by page, and then gives them out to staff, friends and family. The other thing he's been getting done in his office is helping the residence staff make out the shift schedule. Some glitches do occur, but staff know to wink at Emil whenever they want a long paid vacation.

"Hey, Emil," says Maritza, a staff member. "How about a nice paid three-week holiday?"

Emil peers over his glasses. "Okay," he says, smiling. "Sure."

℞

Over the last few months of getting to know Jessie and Emil it has been literally impossible to think of one without the other. They are one entity, one thing, although, of course, they lived separate lives until they came together in Edmonton.

What is known of Jessie's family history is sparse, and most of the connections have just faded away with time and the lack of attention historically paid to the lives of persons with developmental disabilities. She was recently reunited in Vancouver with her brother, Steve, who also has a developmental disability. They've stayed in touch, but Steve, like Jessie, has almost no recollection of their childhood in Drumheller. Nor does he recall much of the time they spent together in Michener Centre from an early age.

Very little else is known about Jessie's family and her early life. She was born on February 12, 1933, married on the 22nd of August, 1987. Asking her about her past simply produces shrugs and smiles.

"So, Jessie, do you remember much about being down in Red Deer, at Michener Centre?"

Shrug. Smile. "I don't know."

"Or about what life was like for you as a little girl?"

Smile. "Don't know."

We do know that Jessie's father's name was Andrew Sawchuk. He passed away twenty years ago. There is no existing information about Jessie's mother. Steve and Jessie have a sister named Kate, but she's rarely been in contact with either of them. She is a nurse and lived for a time near Drumheller. Kate did maintain some contact with Steve for awhile, but after moving from Alberta she failed to send a forwarding address and has not been in contact with Steve or Jessie since then. That was twelve years ago.

Robert and Joyce Brown live in Vancouver, where they have been landlord to and friends with Steve for nearly twenty-five years. They were the ones able to provide this bare amount of information about Jessie's father and sister.

"And that's all we really know," says Joyce Brown. "Steve, like Jessie, is developmentally disabled, and it's not so much that he doesn't remember things, as much as it is he likes to make up stories and can't always tell them apart."

As incredible as it seems, this is really the extent of Jessie's known personal history prior to her move to Edmonton and meeting Emil. To her, the bulk of her past, her 'story', begins with Emil, with meeting and marrying him. Although Emil's personal history is a full and rich one, told easily with humour and love, Jessie's past is cloudy and largely unknown. Still, her present is most certainly clear and sunny. She's with Emil, but she does a lot of other things, too. She spends a fair amount of her time with her volunteer, Reina, who has worked with Jessie for over five years now. They see each other once every couple of weeks. When Reina's mother was ill, before she passed away, Jessie was with Reina all the time, going to the hospital with her, spending time with her.

One thing that Jessie gets a lot of gratification from is the adult support group she attends on Mondays, where she sings and draws. She loves to draw and to have drawings done for her and Emil.

"Do me a drawing of your house," she said to me one visit.

I did my best and then she said, "Now do the back of the house for Mabel."

I did as instructed, and she said, "Look, Mabel. A house. A whole house. One for me and one for you."

Emil took his back-of-the-house drawing to his office. I think he filed it. Jessie coloured hers, and watching her you wonder if she can even imagine living in a house with her very own family. Knowing Jessie, it's clear that before she moved to Edmonton she must have drawn friends to her, and must have had moments of grace and joy with those people. It couldn't be otherwise. But we won't know about such moments in her life. It's not that they didn't happen, but that they are irrecoverable.

Since Jessie left Michener Centre she's learned an enormous number of skills, mostly through informal methods. When she left Michener Centre, for example, she didn't know what a refrigerator was. Now, she contributes around the house with cooking and cleaning, among other things. When she's given positive encouragement and reinforcement, she is a bright and fun person, full of energy and life. She answers the phone around the house and helps out the staff in many other ways. One of the things that is most endearing about Jessie is that if she decides she likes you, an honour in itself, she'll try her hardest to do the right thing for you.

വ

Emil and Jessie have been married for almost thirteen years. This makes Emil a very happy guy, though it is true that he's generally a contented sort of person, pleased with where his life is and where it's been. He's always had great support from his family, particularly his brother Walter and sister Lillian, who are a big part of the lives of both Emil and Jessie.

Emil's family history is wonderfully unique, and in it's immigrant experience, also quintessentially Canadian. Emil is the youngest of nine siblings, five of whom are still alive. His parents emigrated from Russia, but amazingly, the families of both parents came over at different times, when both were small children. The families hailed from the same town in Russia, Volinia, and ended up in the same town in Canada, Bruderheim, but did not know each other back home, though there were distant connections.

"Our mother emigrated with her family in 1902," says Emil's brother, Walter, who is the source of most of the family history. "And our father emigrated with his family in 1907."

These two families came to Canada because of the glowing reports of their predecessors, who'd sent word back that Canada was a good place to live, work and raise a family. And so it was that Emil's mother and father met in Bruderheim as teenagers. They married not long after, and began farming and raising a family, as had Emil's paternal grandparents. Emil was born in 1936, and was in his element on the farm right from the start. He always loved it growing up.

"You could see, though," says Walter, "that he was somewhat slow in developing." Emil was the only child in the family with a developmental disability, and all the other kids loved him from the start. But, being kids, they were also somewhat amused by him. "One thing I always remember," says Walter, "is that as a kid, he could sit in the middle of the floor, his legs stretched out in front of him, put his head on his knees and fall asleep like that. It was incredible."

Emil went to school for a couple of years in Grimsby, a town just outside Bruderheim. This school no longer exists. In those first years it was becoming apparent that Emil's academic progress was stalling. Although his academics may not have been on par, he was developing other skills.

"One thing that Emil loved to do when he was a boy was to play music," says Emil's sister, Lillian. "He couldn't get enough of it. He could recognize tunes, and he loved banging away on the piano, strumming on the guitar. The guitar was actually Walter's, and Walter got so tired of never being able to use it – because Emil always had it – that Walter finally just gave it to him."

While Emil was at school, he got along well with his classmates and teachers, but that wasn't enough to sustain his attendance. Soon Emil left school and began to work at the farm, helping out his dad in any way he could.

"It was a tough life in the 40's and 50's," says Walter. "Mom and Dad worked so hard. But they always cared for Emil. Not that he got an easy ride. I mean, we looked out for him, but he had his jobs to do, too."

Among Emil's many chores were helping with the animals in any number of ways, pumping water from the well for the animals, helping to cook and cleaning the floors of the house. Over the years Emil developed incredibly strong arms from pumping and carrying all the water. His strength served him well, too, when he did eventually go to Michener Centre. There, he worked in the cafeteria, carrying heavy trays in the dining area and around the campus. He was always very proud of the fact that he had the strength and ability to perform these functions, and he took them seriously.

He took his floor cleaning seriously, too, both at Michener Centre and even more so when he was still at home. "Oh, yes," says Lillian, laughing. "You didn't mess with Emil if he'd cleaned the floor. After the rest of us started to have kids, we'd all still go home to visit, but Emil would make sure nobody walked across his clean floor."

"I washed that floor!" Emil would say to the little ones trying to cross. "Don't you step on that floor."

Emil's family weren't the only ones looking out for him on the farm. The family dogs that roamed the acres were probably more protective of Emil than anyone or anything. One day, Emil's mother went out into the farm yard and couldn't find him. She was worried, because Emil usually didn't go that far away from the yard. After looking frantically for a few moments, she found some tracks in the dirt that looked to be about Emil's shoe size. She followed the tracks which led to the road. Half a mile down the gravel highway, she found him, sitting by the roadside, just watching the traffic go by. Sitting on each side of Emil were the two family dogs. They followed Emil everywhere. On this particular day, when Emil decided to wander off and watch traffic, the dogs followed him and stood by him like royal servants, waiting for his next move.

"It was great that Emil was able to grow up on a farm," says Walter. "He was always busy. Dad was patient with him and taught him things. He loved to tie things together, bits of rope and string. He loved the animals, being around them, watching them."

Still, they had to be careful around the animals. When Emil was nine years old, his dad heard barking from the pen where they kept the bull. He went running over to find one of the dogs barking and yapping furiously at the bull, backing it into the far corner of the pen. Emil was standing just outside the pen and there was a large bloody gash on his thigh. Nobody knows exactly what happened. To this day, Emil will not say just how he got that gash, but it's easy, and scary, to imagine.

After Emil's father died in 1962 (he suffered a heart attack while riding his tractor) his mother made the difficult decision to move Emil to Michener Centre. Emil's mother wanted to be sure everything was well with Emil, but, after her husband died, she had to sell the farm, and didn't think she could care for Emil on her own.

"That was very hard for her," says Lillian of their mother. "She was so used to having Emil around, being with him and near him, that it hurt to put him there."

Their mother asked Lillian, Walter and Elmer (another brother, who lives in Drayton Valley) to help her manage things for Emil, and also to make sure that they looked after him when she was gone, even though that was not likely to be for some time. Emil's family is incredibly long-lived, especially on his mother's side of the family. His mother was ninety when she died, his grandma ninety-seven. Emil has had aunts and uncles who have lived to be ninety-six, ninety-four and ninety-one. Other aunts and uncles in their nineties are still alive.

Emil's mother passed away in 1988, and since then Walter has done most of the formal work for Emil as Guardian and Trustee. But Emil has also had the strong support of his sister Lillian and brother Elmer. Together, the three of them have played a large role in making Emil's life a happy and productive one. Their parents always worried a lot about Emil, hoping he would be okay, that he would be well-looked after and that he would not suffer in any way. They were sensitive about not wanting Emil to ever be mistreated in even the smallest way.

"Dad would be so happy today to see Emil, to see the way he is, how his life has gone since 1962. He'd be pleased," says Lillian.

Even at the time of his death, in 1962, Emil's father knew that there was not a lot of understanding about the ways and natures of persons with mental disabilities. "People are starting to understand more, now," says Lillian, "but back then a lot of people didn't. Even families and relatives. We used to live near Alberta Hospital at Oliver, and Dad used to say, 'I don't ever want to see Emil end up at that place, because he's not like that, he's not that way.' Dad would be happy today. Emil's never stopped learning. He's never stopped enjoying things. In fact, he's really only gotten happier."

છ

It's almost a given that we can say the same thing about Jessie as she's gotten older. She's such a strong-minded person, and she has a definite sense of who she is and what she's about. In this, she gets a lot of support from Emil. You can just see it in her eyes that she loves being around Emil, being seen with her husband. Emil gets a lot of satisfaction and pride from supporting Jessie. This comes through in the way they treat one another. Jessie takes the Disabled Adults Transit System (DATS) bus by herself to her Monday class, and is proud of herself for being able to get around on her own. "I've got good brains," she says. "Right Mabel?"

"That's right," says Emil, putting his hand on Jessie's forearm and patting it affectionately.

"That's right," echoes Jessie, smiling back at Emil.

Although she now has a good sense of who she is and what she's about, Jessie can't always tell you how she feels about something, especially anything to do with her past. "Jessie," you might ask, "what was it like growing up around Drumheller? Do you remember anything about the badlands?"

Shrug. Wide smile. "Don't know."

When Jessie is sure of something, though, you'll know it. Especially her sense of people. Once she develops a long-term affection for someone, she is loyal to the extreme. One person, of course, who she is totally loyal to is Emil. She is very consistent and loving and loyal to his family as well. Lillian is very close to the two of them, and probably knows them better than anyone. "The truth," says Lillian, "is that Jessie's just like a sister to me." It's hard not to think that Emil's family fills a big gap in Jessie's life, that gap where we count on our family for support, stability and continuity.

Jessie's happy where she's at right now in her life. She lives an unstructured lifestyle. She likes to go shopping or out for lunch. One of her favorite places to go is Smitty's Restaurant at a nearby mall. Both she and Emil love bacon and eggs. It is one of their favourite meals, and they both love to go to Smitty's and have a nice sitdown meal. All the staff seem to know them, and it's easy to see that a real affection has developed between them and the restaurant staff.

"Hey!" says Jessie to our waitress one day. "Write a hello note to Dawn. Okay? Give Dawn a note, Hello from Jessie. Write that."

The waitress dutifully writes it down and promises to deliver it to Dawn, who isn't scheduled to work until the next day.

"Good," says Jessie, pointing at the note. "You give that to her. Don't forget."

Jessie also has friends in the community whom she maintains contact with, but her number one support is definitely Emil. They take a summer vacation every year. Last year they went to Vancouver and had a great time, visiting Steve and the Browns.

৪৩

Like Jessie, Emil's not much into overplanning his daily activities, but this is exactly the way he wants it. He likes to help out around the house wherever he can, always out of his own initiative and of course, he puts in his office time every day. When his day starts to wind down, Emil generally takes it easy. He doesn't like to go out that much in the evenings, because he's usually a little tired. For the most part Emil is a pretty easygoing sort. He smiles easily, and he likes to watch things happen. He tends to be a bit of an observer, and so he definitely benefits from Jessie's energy and enthusiasm. Looking at Emil, looking at his eyes behind those thick glasses that are forever slipping down on his nose, you just know he's checking things out, watching things, taking it all in. He can be a pretty stubborn guy too, and very single-minded when the mood is on him. When he does happen to get in one of his stubborn moods, he can be a little difficult to reason with, but this rarely happens.

Emil has become friends with the people that live in the duplex, but he tends not to devote as much emotional energy to these friendships as he does to Jessie and his family. He has shown the tendency sometimes to be a bit of a loner, and likes to have time to himself. This need is satisfied through the time he spends in his office. What he really enjoys doing is spending private time with Jessie. He prefers this to spending his recreational time in a large group of friends and peers.

This approach seems to suit Jessie also. They like to spend time together in the evenings, just relaxing. Weekends are spent the way most people spend them. They do some things around the house, and go to church on Sundays. Often, the two of them will go to church with Lillian. Church is very important to both Jessie and Emil.

Lillian has met them at church at least once a month ever since their marriage. She'll meet them for the service – they are Lutheran – and then they go back to Lillian's house for lunch. This is a big part of the lives of Jessie and Emil. Both have a great faith, and both believe very strongly in the power of that faith to support and buoy them.

"God loves Jessie and Mabel," Jessie will tell you if you ask her about her faith. "The devil is the mean one," says Jessie. "Right, Mabel? He's the one that makes you do bad things, and we don't do those things."

Emil's watery eyes take on a serious look. "Yeah. That's right."

And when Jessie wants to confirm that she and Emil are good people, and that they were meant to be together, she will say, "God loves Jessie. Jessie and Mabel."

୫

Jessie and Emil first met at Michener Centre. They got to know one another slowly, mostly as acquaintances. There were many organized social activities at that time for residents, and so Jessie and Emil saw one another on a regular basis, though they lived in different facilities. The residential facilities were divided along gender lines in the 1960s. Emil's family did not actually meet Jessie until Emil had moved to Edmonton, to the residence Jessie happened to be living in. Jessie had obviously been thrilled to see Emil move in to the house. She remembers when he arrived, but only talks about it with a big grin and a sparkle in her eye. "We were going to get married," she says today, meaning she knew it would happen.

It's easy for us to think this is just the hindsight of love, but Lillian confirms Jessie predicted what was going to happen. Lillian will never forget the first time she met Jessie. She and her mother went to the house to visit Emil. He'd been living there about two weeks by this point. When they arrived, Emil's mother went down the hall to Emil's room to see him. Lillian, on the other hand, was stopped in the hall by Jessie, who in her usual enthusiastic way started talking to Lillian. "Mabel and me," she said cheerfully to Lillian, "are going to get married."

"I thought it was the funniest thing," says Lillian now.

"She'd been living in the same house with him for two weeks, and here she was saying she was going to marry him. But every single time I went over there, for a year after, she would tell me that her and Emil were going to get married. She was always so friendly and cheerful when she said it. And she was right, too."

Jessie still likes to tell the story herself of how she and Emil got together. She tells it slightly differently than Lillian, but the decision-making process seems just as swift. Emil was the one, no ands, ifs or buts. They were at church one Sunday. "I had some wine," says Jessie, "at the church, and it made me a bit sick. I felt sick and then I fell down. I hit my head and my nose bled. But Mabel was right behind me. He picked me up. Right away." A smile crosses Jessie's face and she touches Emil as she tells the story. "And I thought, 'This is a pretty nice guy.' I married him."

℘

Of course, the reality of making it happen wasn't quite that easy. To begin with, Emil's mother was skeptical. As much as she loved her son, she still considered him a grown man with a child's mind. After awhile however, she began to see that Jessie and Emil were together a lot, and that every time the family wanted to do something with Emil, he wanted to bring Jessie along. One thing that made Emil's family sit up and take notice, was that Emil, who had always been a silent person, was starting to speak more often, and more clearly.

"Jessie really is so ideal for Emil," says Lillian. "And vice versa. It's like they actually think for each other. And because Jessie likes to talk and Emil still doesn't talk all that much, she can often say what he's thinking, and somehow it is always

113

exactly what he's thinking. Sometimes I think they read each others' minds."

Jessie is certainly the more proactive of the two. She likes to do things, to get out, to be active. She's been great for Emil in that way. But even when Emil would rather stay around to tend the home fires, Jessie still does things on her own, such as her Monday classes, where they do the drawing and singing.

"I sing good," she says happily.

I look over to Emil. "Is that right, Emil? Do you like to hear Jessie sing?"

Emil lets a smile just creep onto his face. "Yeah," he says slyly. "Sometimes."

Jessie cackles with delight. They like to joke with each other. Emil got Jessie a nightgown at Christmas, and Jessie wears it because she feels so comfortable. "It keeps me warm at nights," says Jessie. Emil, his voice dry and sarcastic, says, "Yeah, keeps me warm, too."

Their relationship is smooth now, but the start was difficult in that they had so many taboos to break through, so many preconceptions to fight. Some of the biggest were the preconceptions of Emil's own family. Emil's mother, who always liked Jessie very much, was still concerned about the idea of them being together. Her main concern was their stability. Would they last? What would happen if they broke up? What about all the legalities? And more than anything else, what about their sensitivities, their vulnerabilities? She wondered if they were more susceptible to being hurt than people without developmental disabilities.

One of the things that gave Emil's family a much greater comfort level during the time when Jessie and Emil began seriously considering marriage was the input of their support staff. The staff often remarked upon how much Jessie and Emil seemed in tune with one another, how they had an understanding of one another beyond anything the staff had ever seen before in a relationship in the general population, let alone the population of persons with mental disabilities.

Their commitment to one another also continually impressed those around them. "Emil was always insisting Jessie be a part of things," says Lillian, with a smile. It became more and more obvious that they were extremely close, nearly inseparable. "And just the fact that she can say so much of what is on Emil's mind. That always stuck out for us."

As Jessie and Emil began to get close in those early years of living in the same residence, the rest of Emil's family noticed that Emil, too, began talking about getting married. Of course, Jessie had always talked about it, but after they had lived in the Westmount residence for a couple of years together, Emil actually began to echo the marriage talk. He'd seen all his siblings get married, have weddings, be happy with someone else. He knew, says Lillian, what the concept of marriage meant, and what it meant to make a commitment to someone else.

Still, Emil's mother was not entirely comfortable. Lillian remembers talking to her husband about it at the time. "I remember saying to him, 'What would happen to them if they were separated?' You know, what would become of them if they didn't make their relationships formal, and somehow they got moved to different facilities or something?" Encouraging them to get married would prevent that. They were simply meant to be together.

Lillian talked it over with her mother, who gradually

overcame her worry and skepticism. Walter believes their mother, who was 89 at the time of the wedding, was literally staying alive to ensure that Emil would be taken care of. Once she was comfortable with things, once she saw for certain how much this meant to Emil and his happiness, she then felt she'd completed her life's work of raising her family. Emil and Jessie were married in 1987. Emil's mother passed away the next year at the age of 90.

"She loved Emil so much," says Lillian. "She was maybe a little over protective of him, a little selfish even, when it came to him marrying Jessie. All her life she'd had his affections, and maybe it was a bit hard for her to think that that affection was going somewhere else."

Even though the family was now supportive and enthusiastic, the wedding still almost didn't happen. The problem now was the government. There was virtually no precedent for such weddings to take place, a staggering thought considering that this was 1987. The government informed Jessie and Emil that they were insufficiently capable of understanding the meaning of marriage, and therefore were not allowed to obtain a legal marriage licence. This caused sadness for Jessie and Emil, and great indignation amongst everybody associated with them. They knew they wanted to live together and be together, but the formal recognition of it was important, too. Emil and Jessie wanted to be officially married. Emil had such respect for his siblings and he wanted to do what they had done. Emil's mother, now fully supportive of the marriage, spoke to Pastor Kentel at the Stony Plain Lutheran Church. He agreed to meet with Jessie and Emil.

Agency staff also arranged an interview with a doctor, so

that the physician could discuss with Jessie and Emil their understanding of marriage. Lillian says the agency staff have been excellent throughout the years for both Jessie and Emil, and that the staff were instrumental in helping make the marriage happen.

The physician met with Jessie and Emil. After a long discussion, he told them he thought that they most certainly did understand what marriage meant. They fully understood, he said, what would be the joys and difficulties of the commitment they wanted to make. The physician immediately consented to sign a marriage licence for them.

While this was going on, Jessie and Emil met with Pastor Kentel in Stony Plain. After meeting with Jessie and Emil, he agreed to marry them, whether they had a licence or not. They ought to be married, he said. And he wanted to do the service.

The wedding was planned for August 22, 1987 – a full service, to be followed by a banquet and dance. The formal wedding licence arrived just one week before the ceremony. Jessie and Emil approached the date with great excitement. The day itself is one nobody will ever forget. Lillian has the ceremony and reception on tape, and the joy on the faces of Jessie and Emil is clear. Emil was in his tux, Jessie in her beautiful gown.

"It was a really nice day," says Jessie, remembering it, grinning, still proud. Emil points at Jessie and smiles his slow smile. "She had on a nice blue dress." Together, they have great memories of the wedding, and it still brings them joy to think about it.

"You should have seen everybody," says Lillian. "You will never see a happier collection of people." Along with family and all the staff they knew, Jessie and Emil had also invited the many friends they'd made over the years from Michener Centre and the Westmount residence. The mood was joyous and more than anything it was just a great party. But you can also see on the faces of people in attendance that it was more than that, that the day had a certain special meaning for many people other than Jessie and Emil. That day, August 22, 1987, was also a celebration of the real meaning of owning a life, of having responsibility and individuality.

Jessie and Emil have developmental disabilities. This is true. But they are whole, unique people, with joys and sorrows, faults and good points, bad days and good days. They are in the world, and are not separate from it, nor should they be separated from it. On their wedding day, they not only said "I love you," to one another, but they said "Yes" to being in the world. It was a great day, and you could see as much on the faces of their friends gathered there. They accepted the world, even though the world still struggles to accept Jessie and Emil as equals.

"Jessie and Emil's marriage has turned out so well," says Walter. "They're both a lot happier than they would have been otherwise. Either one would do anything for the other. You can see that just by looking at them."

જી

If you are lucky enough to spend any time at all with Jessie and Emil, one thing you will learn is that they love to dance. Every week they attend a dance at the ACT centre down in Edmonton's Rundle Park. There is live dancehall music, usually provided by a local volunteer band. To see Jessie and Emil dancing is to revisit the first time you ever did a thing and enjoyed it so much you were conscious of nothing else. That's the way it is for Jessie and Emil. They love to dance. They love to be with one another.

While the musicians are setting up, Emil likes to stand near the front of the room. He won't sit down. He wants to be ready, so that he doesn't miss a minute of available dancing time. Emil wants to be treated like a person who can and will do the things for himself that he wants to do. Someone who treats him differently will hear about it. Emil has a strong sense of who he is, and he inspires respect in people. Standing up at the front, watching things unfold before the music starts, he almost looks like a conductor waiting for his entrance.

Jessie, meanwhile, is up talking to the musicians while they set up their stands. "Hi," she says, smiling away. "I'm Jessie. I'm dancing today."

The musicians smile back and keep setting up their instruments, deciding the order of songs. "Great," they say back to Jessie. "We'll do what we can to play songs you like."

"Yeah," says Jessie enthusiastically. She goes closer to Emil. "Mabel! They said they're going to play songs we like."

Emil smiles. "Yeah."

The music starts and they're on the floor. Emil holds Jessie with grace and care, not going too fast. Jessie has complained about a sore toe this day, but she seems to have forgotten that. Every now and then she looks around to smile at people she knows, and her smile is clearly indicating a message. "I'm so happy to be dancing with my husband." You can't help but smile back at her.

Emil, meanwhile, is concentrating. He's a good dancer, in control, and you can tell he takes his duty to lead seriously.

Watching them dance, it's easy to see the love. The phrase "love story" is one Jessie has picked up on. She likes to use it to describe herself and Emil. Knowing that someone was interested in their story, in making sure their story got told, Jessie became vocal in her pride, as did Emil, though in a quieter way. Jessie became curious about it all, asking every time I visit.

"It's a love story, me and Mabel," she said to me. She looked to Emil. "Isn't that right, Mabel?"

"Yeah," said Emil, nodding, peering at us through those coke-bottle lenses, giving us a contented little grin. "That's right."

"When are you going to finish?" said Jessie. "When are you going to be done our love story?"

"Soon."

Then Jessie asked the most revealing question, a question that underlined the first forty years of her life, years of not being allowed to own even the most basic information and stories and facts that have made up who she is and what she has lived. "Can we look at it when it's done? Are Jessie and Mabel going to be allowed to see it?"

"Of course, you can. It's about you two. It's your story."

Jessie leaned over and peered into Emil's face. "Hear that Mabel. We get to see our love story."

I don't have glasses, but if I did, if I had big glasses like Emil's, they'd have fogged over. "That's right," I said. "Because it's yours."

Emil's sweet knowing grin spreads slowly over his face. "Yeah," he said, pausing to savour the sound of the words. "Our love story."

Jessie and Emil Kupsch

Photo by Sears™, 1999

Winter

If you enjoyed **Someone Like That** and would like to purchase additional copies for friends, family or colleagues, send us a cheque or money order along with the order form below.

[   ] YES, I would like __ copies of **Someone Like That** at $16.95 each.

[   ] YES, I would like __ copies of the limited edition print of the cover art by Nina Haggerty* at $50.00 each.

Total $ _____

Shipping and Handling (Books)
(1-3 copies, $3.00; 4-6 copies $5.00; 7 or more,
please phone for details and discounts)
Shipping and Handling (Posters)
($5.00 each) $ _____

GST 7% $ _____

TOTAL ENCLOSED $ _____

* Limited Edition Prints of other art by Nina Haggerty may also be available upon request.

Please make cheques payable to:
Rowan Books

Name: _____

Organization: _____

Address: _____

Prov/State: _____

Postal Code: _____

Phone: _____ email: _____

Send orders with cheque or money order enclosed to:
Rowan Books
#410, 10113 - 104 St.
Edmonton, AB
T5J 1A1
Phone: (780)421-1544 Fax: (780)421-1588 email: jonrach@msn.com

For bulk orders and fundraising options, please contact Rowan Books.